JOURNEYING TO MY TRUEST IDENTITY

BECOMING THE ME GOD CREATED

by

JOYCE KELLY-LEWIS, PhD, MSW

JOURNEYING TO MY TRUEST IDENTITY

Joyce Kelly- Lewis, PhD, MSW.

All Scriptures used are cited individually and were taken from Bible Gateway at https//biblegateway.com. The different translations used were The Passion Translation, The Message, Easy-to-Read Version, New King James Version, and New International Version,

With one exception, all names used are fictitious to protect the identity of individuals. The exception is Dr. Thomas and Mrs. Hope Norman. Their names were used with permission from their daughter.

The profits from the sale of this book support Bethel Atlanta Africa (bethelatlantaafrica.com) projects and New Life Church Community Center (newlife-atl.org). Thank you for support.

Website: www.joycekellylewis.com

DEDICATION

This book is dedicated to the loving memory of my four siblings who died in 2018 and 2019:

James Ellis Kelly Sr. – April 6, 1937 – Jan. 6, 2018

Dr. Rev. Willie Lee Kelly – Dec. 28, 1945 – Dec. 19, 2018

Doris Jean Kelly-Beasley – April 7, 1935 – Jan. 25, 2019

Alberta Delores Kelly-Blanks – Oct. 28, 1948 – Jul 9, 2019

And three other siblings who died in earlier years:

Rev. Cleophus Kelly – Jul 14, 1932 – Oct. 10, 1968

Rev. Don Albert Kelly – May 30, 1942 – June 30, 1992

Rev. Napolean Kelly – May 26, 1931 – Dec. 12, 2007

There were fourteen who lived to adulthood, and now there are seven.

You're sorely missed. Thank you for the life lessons each one of you taught me. I think of you when I use the lessons. I find great comfort in knowing you knew and had a relationship with God.

3

ACKNOWLEDGMENTS

Thank You God for giving me the assignment to write, and for the blessed assurance that I could do it. I didn't want to write this book about my life for many reasons, but I knew I had to obey God. However, it did take me a minute or two (actually years) to complete this book from the time I got the assignment.

I'm so happy God is patient with me. As I was doing the final edit, I was reminded of the many trials I've come through in life by the grace of God. I've experienced lots of healing and learned lessons I believe God wanted me to share. I was also reminded of the favor God has placed on my life.

My husband, Robert, is acknowledged for his willingness to read and offer feedback many times as I was writing. Thank you for being kind with your comments. My writing partner, Tresha Jackson was very helpful as we sat and discussed my progress or lack thereof – thank you. My three daughters: Joy, Sherri, and Kelli offered me valuable advice as I was working on this project. Hearing from you, "Mom this is good" meant so much to me, especially since you're awesome writers. Sherri, your advice as an author and editor was invaluable. My daughters are the best.

Thank you to the siblings who encouraged me to write this book. One told me, "It will help you and others when you write it." Your encouragement meant a lot to me.

To all my grands, I thank God you're in my life. Jordan, I want to thank you for being a wonderful granddaughter to me and Papa. I love reading your writings. The technological help you give is invaluable. You're so gifted. I'm encouraged by you. My boys, Ahav and Analiel, you are a gift from God to me. I love how you help when I'm making up and telling you stories. This keeps me using my mind to imagine far out things; it enhances my story telling and writing for children. Elvira, you came into my life six years ago; it has been enriched by you. You are a young lady full of dreams that you will fulfill one day.

Thanks,

Joyce

CONTENTS

"I believe that within each of us lies the deep desire and the capacity to do something great with our lives. I refuse to settle for anything less than the greatness I was born for – the greatness God ordained for me before I was even born."

Sherri Lewis

INTRODUCTION

The emotional pain that results from the experiences of living and operating in the American culture as a Black woman can, at times, be overwhelming. We are often caught off guard by traumatic experiences and work to find a way to just get through. Masking your emotions can become a very common response to handling this pain. However, continued masking can interfere with you remaining authentic and true to yourself.

This book is written for Black women of the African diaspora who want to take the journey to their truest identity. I was given an assignment by God to share information about my life journey to encourage other women to begin the journey to their truest self.

This is a purposeful journey. You will learn to identify and rid yourself of lies you've learned to believe about yourself, and pains of the past. The true you can then become skilled at handling emotional pain in a healthy manner and you won't need to wear masks. You will be enabled to walk in destiny and carry out your purpose in life.

After I share about my beginnings in Chapter One, Chapter Two begins with the question, "Where are you?" The book ends with the chapter, "Am I There Yet?" Between the beginning and ending chapters, you are invited to read about my journey and its challenges. I ask that you allow my story to propel you to start your journey to your authentic self. I believe this is one of, if not, the most important journey you will take in your life.

This book contains exercises at the end of each chapter. The exercises called, "It's Your Turn," invite you to reflect on what you have read, see if you can relate to the situation or experience, and then write down what you've learned about you. The next exercise, "What Do I Do Now?" will assist you in developing ways to incorporate the learning into your daily life. You will write down the things you will practice, practice, and practice until they become a part of you.

Throughout this book, I'll be asking you to ask questions of the Holy Spirit to get insight into many things. The Holy Spirit knows you better than anyone and can help you identify the things that keep you stuck, the lies you believe about yourself, and the pain from the past that needs to be healed.

It's easy to hear from God. When you do the exercise, quiet yourself and then listen to that still small Voice within. You'll be surprised at how easy it is to hear Him and the truths He's able to reveal to you as you journey toward healing and identity.

I want you to engage as many of your six senses as possible as you read this book: smell, taste, hearing, touch, sight, and common sense. Get your pen and journal, and remember, this is a journey, not a destination. We are searching for and asking God to reveal your truest identity:

I-Identify where you are now

D-Decide how you got to this point; describe your journey thus far

E-Enlist the help of others in identifying blind spots

N-Note lies that have become your truths; replace with God's truths

T-Think about changing negative thoughts and behaviors

I-Inform one other trustworthy person of your intentions (an accountability partner)

T-Transformation is coming

Y-Yield your journey and destiny to God

Are you ready? Let's go.

IT'S YOUR TURN

Your first assignment is to pray the prayer below. After praying it, I want you to then write your own prayer. Tell God what you want to happen for you as a result of reading this book and doing the exercises. Pray your written prayer before and after each chapter. Add your gratitude for the changes you experience along the way.

Dear Father God, Daddy, Abba,

Thank You for this opportunity to come before You as Your child. I am ready and willing to pull back the curtains of time and memories, so the lies of the enemy can be exposed. I know the lies and hurts from the past must be exposed so You can heal me.

I thank You because You want me healed, delivered, and whole. I am ready for the journey to the real me, the person You have called me to be.

Jesus, guard my heart as I open myself for examination. Holy Spirit, show me how to receive Your revelations about the strongholds in my life that have produced fear, low self-esteem, destructive behaviors, anger, and the inability to trust You and others.

Show me whatever keeps me bound and off track. Please, show me if I have built walls of protection in the past, so I could survive in my environment. Holy Spirit, Daddy, and Jesus, I ask that

11

You show me You are here with me every step of the way as I do journey work.

I thank You. I praise You. In Jesus' name I pray.

Amen.

IT'S YOUR TURN

Write Your Prayer Here

Tell God what you want to happen as you do journey work. Thank Him for blessing you on the journey to your truest identity. Revisit this prayer often. You can come back and add to it at any time.

Those who trust in the Lord are as unshakeable,
as unmovable as mighty Mount Zion!
Just as the mountains surround Jerusalem,
so the Lord's wrap-around presence
surrounds his people, protecting them now and
forever.

Psalm 125:1-2 (TPT)

CHAPTER 1

My Early Journey

I want to take you on a walk through my life. I'm doing this so you can glean from my journey, and gain wisdom for your own. I'm being vulnerable and authentic as I take you deep into my life story. I want you to learn from my story as you begin journeying to your truest identity.

I want to paint a picture of my childhood so you can see where I started, and the difficulties I've encountered, so you can celebrate with me where I am today. It's hard to believe what my life has become based on where I started. Now, I'm happily married for over fifty years, I raised two daughters who are doctors, and one who is an artist. I've earned a PhD and became a college professor. Now, I'm an author.

When you read my story, you'll see why I paint a picture for you. If I could come through what I've come through to get to where I am today, so can you. I want you to see and understand that no matter where you are presently, you can make it to your truest identity as I did.

My life began in College Station, Arkansas in a home with my parents and eight older siblings. I was born at home – the ninth child of sixteen live births. Fourteen of us lived to adulthood – seven boys and seven girls. A boy and girl had died in infancy. My family lived in a three-bedroom wooden-framed house – one bedroom for my parents, one for the girls, and one for the boys. There were two double beds in each of the children's rooms.

This predominantly black community on the outskirts of Little Rock, Arkansas was not urban, and yet it was not rural. There was a paved road that went from one end of the community to the other. The side roads were not paved. There was no electricity, running water, or indoor plumbing. We used kerosene lamps, drew water from a well, and used an outhouse.

There were five grocery stores in the community, all owned by whites. We would charge basic groceries there – flour, meal, sugar, lard, and sometimes meat. We never seemed to pay off the grocery bills. That's the way it was in the day, and it was accepted. People were happy they were allowed credit so they could purchase necessary items.

My father worked at a lumber mill and later became a pastor. My mother was a housewife, so we didn't have much income. We were a very large, poor family. When we told the next generation the story of how we grew up, one nephew remarked, "You weren't poor. You were po'. You couldn't afford the 'or' to spell poor." A brother, in his humorous way, said, "We were so poor the church mice could've donated to us."

To help our children understand just how poor we were, we told them about our dump experiences. We would go to the city dump to dig through rubbish to find clothes, shoes and other usable items. We also got food from the dump.

Families would get to the dump early and stake out an area to dig through the rubbish looking for treasures. We had two families as digging partners. We would assist each other in finding a match to a shoe, different sized clothing, etc. If you found a shoe, you'd hold it up and yell, "Anyone see a match?" The family's digging partners would assist in finding the other shoe.

We stayed out of school to meet the food trucks that dumped meat, ice cream, baked goods, and expired foods from local grocery stores. We knew the dumping schedules of the different trucks, so we would get there to catch the food as it was being dumped. The drivers were nice. They would dump the food slowly so we could catch it before it hit the ground, or the dump workers covered it. If you weren't there to catch the food, you could always dig for it.

To this day, our children still have difficulty believing and accepting our dump experiences, especially our getting food from it.

We raised chickens, pigs and cows at our home. The hogs were raised for our meat. Killing day was always interesting to me as a child because of what we could do with the various parts of the hogs. Once the hogs were killed and cleaned, we made lard and pork skins from the pig's skin and fatty layer. We made chitterlings from the intestines, hog head souse from the head, pickled pigs' feet from the feet. There was very little waste.

The big, black all-purpose pot in the backyard was used to make lye soap. The soap was used for bathing, washing, and doing dishes. That big black pot was also used to heat water for hog killing and baths, making crackling, and to soak dirty clothes.

We milked the cows daily. Some of the milk was for drinking, the other was placed in a churn for butter and buttermilk. The buttermilk was sometimes combined with cornbread for dinner.

We had a large vegetable garden with some of the best tasting veggies. I still remember going to the garden, picking tomatoes and eating them directly off the vines. The greens were cooked with fatback from the hogs we had slaughtered. When you added cornbread with the greens, you had dinner.

Our living conditions contributed to us becoming a creative group of children. We didn't have toys, so we created our own. For example, we took empty tin cans, put holes in the unopened end, pulled a cord through them, then walked on them. We would take a newspaper, get under the porch with a flashlight, and create a movie and cartoons. The game of jacks was played with all rocks, no ball or jacks.

This creativity we had as children has continued to show up in our adulthood in a variety of ways. There are bakers, seamstresses, pastors, builders, business owners, singers, musicians, cosmetologists, educators, and a body care product maker. As adults, some of us talk about the talent in the family and where we would be if we'd had guidance and direction during critical developmental periods in our lives.

College Station was a good place to find people eager to work. Trucks came through the community to take people to the cotton fields. The trucks were big with an open back and a tarp over it. The owner outfitted the truck with benches for you to sit on if you got on the truck early. Otherwise you were packed in and stood for the entire trip to the cotton field. The truck owner got a fee for every worker he delivered. One truck owner always wanted to make sure my siblings and I were on his truck because we were responsible workers.

Children in my family started working at early ages. We worked hard at home, and in the fields for white farmers. We chopped cotton in the blistering sun, and picked cotton when the bolls were ready. Towards the end of the cotton season, we pulled cotton that had been left from the first picking. As we got older, some of my brothers went to work in a lumber mill with my father, and in butcher shops. The girls worked as maids. These were the jobs available to us then.

We had one school in our community which served grades one through eight. There was one classroom for each grade level. The small, wooden building had no running water or indoor plumbing. We walked at least two miles to school in the heat and in the cold.

There was no high school in College Station for blacks, so we had to ride a school bus about twelve miles away. The high school served Blacks in at least five different rural communities. The school offered courses to earn the sixteen credits needed to graduate; there were no electives.

Our school systems were legally segregated. They were reported to be separate but equal. However, we got the throw-a-ways from the white schools. The books were severely worn, sometimes with no covers. The desks were carved with names and other graffiti. There was no library at any grade level, no real playgrounds at elementary schools, and no labs at the high school (until I moved to the city). There were no attendance laws for the "colored students," as we were called then.

Some of our teachers were called in-service teachers, because they didn't have a college degree. They taught school during the regular school year and went to college in the summer to complete their degree. However, they really cared about students' learning and were adamant about teaching us what they knew. I realized, as an adult and parent of school-aged children, how much information was missing from my education in a segregated school system.

Sending children to school was not a priority for my parents. During the cotton picking season, we were sent to school only when it rained. Otherwise, we were in the fields until the crops were harvested. Needless to say, I wasn't getting the best education. When I was in the eighth grade, my principal, who was also the English teacher, said to me, "I wonder what kind of student you'd be if you came to school on a regular basis. As it is, you're making good grades on my tests." He put my test paper on my desk. It had a big "A" on it.

One of my older brothers begged my parents repeatedly to let me go to school rather than work in the fields. He told them, "She's smart and she needs to go to school." He promised them he would do extra work in the field to make up for my not going. They did not honor his request, so I continued to be a "field hand." My parents weren't educated, so this probably influenced their views on education.

My parents were very controlling. When they told you to do something, you did it because they had a way of instilling fear in you. They also required that you "not think for yourself." My mother often told me, "You think you have a mind of your own." This happened when I was attempting to express myself.

I would answer her with, "Yes, God gave each one of us a mind of our own." This exchange usually ended in a beating for me. I often wondered what caused my parents to be the way they were and to do what they did.

There were so many restrictions about where we could go and what we could do. I was not allowed to do "normal" child and teenage activities like dancing, dating, or just hanging out with friends. I didn't even attend my senior prom or banquet. I was told these things were sins, and I was a sinner for wanting to do them. You can't begin to imagine the shame this causes for a child or teen.

My parents had two sides – a public and a private one. When I heard people talk about them publicly, I always wondered, *who are they talking about?* Or I would think, *if only you knew what went on behind closed doors.* My parents enforced strict rules to ensure family secrets stayed inside the home. I have learned family secrets can destroy families over time because of the mistrust that develops.

I worked to maintain my individuality in the family, even though it was hard and costly. I always saw myself as different growing up. I was so different I convinced myself I was adopted – not a real member of the family. I now know that was one of my strategies for surviving in my biological family.

When I look at the past and see how far I've come, I try to identify people who inspired me along the way. There was the Sunday School teacher who allowed me to help her teach the class and review the lesson during the general assembly of all classes. I was chosen because I could remember what had been taught and memorize Scriptures to recite.

My Home Economics teacher in ninth grade hired me to help her sew. She was a very fashionable lady who tailored all her clothes. I felt special because I was chosen from all her students and got paid fifty cents each time I helped her. That was a lot of money for a poor teen. Going into her home and seeing how she lived offered me a very different view of how a person could live.

My family moved to Little Rock when I was a senior in high school. I attended Horace Mann High School which was different from my country school. There were electives, a chemistry laboratory, and more courses than I had ever heard of before. I was like a kid in a candy store. I took lots of courses that were not offered at my old school – Chemistry, Trigonometry, Solid Geometry, and Negro History.

My twelfth grade Chemistry teacher saw something in me I wasn't ready to see in myself. He gave me extra experiments in the lab (my new school had a lab), and put me in charge when he had to leave class to handle a discipline problem. He was both teacher and vice-principal. I always got B's in his class. In later years, when I visited him, he greeted me with, "Kelly, my only A student" (he called me Kelly, rather than Joyce). I told him I never got an A in his class. He told me, "You earned it; I just didn't give it to you."

At Horace Mann, I attended my first career day. I heard about more careers than I could've ever imagined. The only careers I knew about before then were pastoring, teaching, medicine, and nursing. I learned about medical technology at the career day.

When I graduated from high school at barely seventeen, I thought I would automatically go to college in the fall. I had always said I was going to be a doctor, and my parents knew I wanted to go to college. I was so disappointed when I found out my parents had not made arrangements for and had no intentions of me going to college. They said they needed me to work to help support the family rather than go to college.

I was so intent on going to college that I worked during the day and went to a small black college at night. I found a job as a maid for a family of six, and worked five full days a week. I caught the bus with the other maids in the morning to ride to "The Heights," an affluent, all-white area. After I began working there, I realized I wanted to as live in an area like the Heights, not work there as a maid.

After three years of college, my journey took me from an all-black environment to a predominately white world when I entered Medical Technology School at the University of Arkansas Medical

Sciences Campus (UAMS). I couldn't begin to imagine the changes I would need to make to survive in that environment. The setting wasn't conducive for someone like me – black, female, smart, from a poor community, and determined to succeed no matter what they did to prevent me.

There were extra obstacles in the educational arena for me and other Blacks to deal with in the programs offered at UAMS. The biggest obstacle we faced was racism. It began for me in the interview to get into the program. The interview focused on what I would do if I wasn't successful in the program and had other negative questions. On the bus ride home after the interview, all I could think about was the director's questions and discouraging comments.

Her comments had such a negative impact on me, I began to doubt if I would be accepted into the program, even though I met the requirements. One of my recommendations came from the Chief of Pathology, Dr. Norman. I was working in his laboratory when I applied to the program. The school of Medical Technology was under Pathology at the time. How do you not accept someone the department head had recommended?

Later, I could see God in the plan for my life. His Word says, "For I know the plans I have for you, declares the Lord, plans to prosper you and not to harm you, plans to give you hope and a future."

(Jeremiah 29:11, NIV). I experienced the goodness of God even when working as a maid.

I didn't like working as a maid. However, when I look back, it was a key position for the next phase of my life. I went from being a maid in the Norman home to being an assistant in Dr. Norman's laboratory. The Normans later told me that they could tell I wasn't meant to be a maid because I carried books to study on the bus ride to and from work.

The Normans were a Christian family who cared about my well-being and wanted to know my plans for the future. Mrs. Norman gave me clothes so I could dress decently. I got exposed to and learned so much while working in that household and in the lab. The learning helped prepare me for the next phase of my educational journey.

I got married while getting my degree in Medical Technology and before applying to medical school. My husband was in his third year of medical school. We got married on a Saturday and were back in class on Monday. Finishing school and settling into a new marriage was an exciting, yet stressful leg of my journey.

We had a very simple wedding ceremony at my home since we were students with no real money. I had a maid of honor and Robert had a best man. The minister married us for free because he knew we were struggling students. My parents, his grandmother (who had raised him) and other family members were in attendance. Mrs. Norman also attended our wedding.

While students at UAMS, we were denied student housing. No blacks were allowed to live in the dormitories. We didn't challenge this policy. I guess we were happy to have been accepted into our respective programs. There was a Black lady near the medical school who allowed us to rent an attic room for forty dollars a month. We had a bed at one end, a small sofa at the other end, and a chest of drawers. We were thankful for the space and the price.

Robert and I graduated from our respective programs in 1966. We left Arkansas for Philadelphia for his medical internship in the Navy. I worked in the special chemistry laboratory at the Hospital of the University of Pennsylvania. We left Arkansas believing we were going to the "City of Brotherly Love." We had expected to face less discrimination than we had in our home state. We were sorely mistaken.

Robert was the first of his intern group to arrive in Philadelphia to begin apartment hunting. What an experience. We received a list of available apartments near the hospital. I made appointments to see the apartments. When we arrived and they saw we were Black, we were told the apartments had been rented. This continued at one apartment after another.

We were even denied an apartment in a complex where the Navy subsidized the rent for interns. We later found that many of the white interns got an apartment in this complex and many of the other places where we had been denied an apartment, even though we had arrived weeks before them.

The interns living in the Navy subsidized apartments thought we should've contested the denial. We chose not to question the disparities. When I look back on how easily we accepted the housing denials "in the day," it appears life had taught us not to question the system. You just do what you were there to accomplish, then leave.

Once my husband became a doctor, he told me his views on his wife working outside of the home. He had grown up believing he would become a good provider so his wife wouldn't have to work. Seeing how his mother, grandmother, and other black women had worked hard in and outside the home had greatly influenced him. He wanted me to be a stay-at-home wife and mother.

Staying at home was counter to what I wanted. I wanted a career. I wanted to experience working as a professional. However, I gave in to my husband's wishes. This was the second detour from my "Plan A".

Life as a stay-at-home wife and mother was not easy because I felt there was so much I was supposed to do. I became a homemaker who could've outshone June Cleaver of *Leave it to Beaver*. I baked everything from scratch including breads, pies and cakes; cooked both soul food and gourmet meals; sewed clothes, drapery, and bedspreads, wall-papered and painted rooms. I took great care of my family.

In my "spare time," I took up different hobbies, ones I had never heard of growing up, nor envisioned I would participate in. I learned to play golf and tennis, took up painting, woodworking, and ceramics. I also participated in different craft classes at church. I was surprised to discover how well I did in all the activities. I didn't have a clue that I could be so creative. You could say I learned how to play in adulthood.

The churches we attended over the years enlisted me as a Sunday School teacher and youth group leader. Our home became the place for youth to come, talk, and get advice. I became more of a people person and participated in artsy activities.

I had gotten off the path I had planned before getting married and having children, and I didn't have a plan B. While staying at home, I had to make changes so that I could adjust to the so-called easy life of a stay-at-home wife and mother.

After being a stay-at-home mother and participating in new and different activities, I changed. I was no longer the left-brained person interested in the sciences. I wasn't sure of who I had become. I just knew I had become a different person. It was time for me to do an assessment.

IT'S YOUR TURN

Looking Back At Life

Complete this form.

The family that I was born into had ___ people. List the names of your family members.

1. _____

2. _____

3. _____

4. _____

5. _____

6. _____

7. _____

My family lived in (describe the living quarters and area where you lived)

_____

_____

What was your position in the family – oldest, youngest, or middle? How did this position in the family affect you?

31

_____

_____

Who did the nurturing in your family?

_____

What values were taught in your home? Who did the teaching? How was the teaching done?

_____

_____

_____

_____

Were there unspoken messages in your home? What were they?

_____

_____

What "lessons for life" did you learn from growing up in your home?

_____

_____

Are there some lessons you learned that you would like to discard?

_____

_____

Describe the "you" that resulted from growing up in your family.

_____

_____

_____

NOTES:

_____

_____

_____

_____

_____

_____

_____

WHAT DO I DO NOW?

Now that you've looked back on your family and see the things learned, I want you to write a story about your life. Who were the influencers in your life? Who were the go-to-people in your life? Were these people outside or inside your family? I want you to be authentic and transparent as you write your story. You may want to continue writing your story in your journal.

_____

_____

_____

_____

_____

_____

_____

_____

_____

_____

_____

And I find that the strength of Christ's explosive power infuses me to conquer every difficulty.

Philippians 4:13 (TPT)

God, I invite your searching gaze into my heart. Examine me through and through; find out everything that may be hidden within me. Put me to the test and sift through all my anxious cares. See if there is any path of pain I'm walking on, and lead me back to your glorious, everlasting ways—the path that brings me back to you.

Psalm 139:23-24 (TPT)

CHAPTER 2

Checking In: An Assessment

The journey to your truest identity begins with an assessment of where you are presently. To assess or examine ourselves is not to judge and condemn. It's just an exercise to locate where you are. It's to identify if you have gotten away from God and His purpose for your life. This assessment will require you to ask God for a thorough search. I did this assessment years ago and was amazed to discover how I had allowed life events to take me off course and away from *me*. I will guide you through a "checking in" process to determine where you are as compared to where you thought you'd be.

There's a quote I've kept in my personal folder since the 1980's. It reads, "I'm Lost – I've gone to look for myself. If I should return before I get back, please ask me to wait." This statement was so true for me when I got serious about journey work. Life circumstances can take you so far off course that you may not recognize who you are or where you are on your journey.

It's as if one day, you wake up, don't recognize who you are, and begin to question yourself. Who have I become? Where am I? How did I get here? What took me off course? How did this happen?

Was I not paying attention to the paths I was taking? There appears to be an unseen art to losing oneself.

Here's an example. Have you gone to a mall to shop at a particular store, and then realized you didn't know where it was located or how to get there? You wander around a bit, and then see the mall map. The first thing that you notice is a big X that says, "You are here." From there, you can locate the store you want.

Let's apply this example to life. What happens if or when you get lost on life's journey and can't find your way? Is there a map to help you get back on track? Is there someone you can ask for directions? Even more importantly, do you recognize that you're lost and if so, do you want to get back on track?

I didn't have a good journey map, or a mentor telling me how to get from where I was to where I wanted to go – from a small impoverished town to medical school. I didn't believe I could afford medical school because I wasn't knowledgeable about resources. However, it wasn't just about the lack of sufficient funds. I was also missing out because of a lack of exposure. One thing I've learned in my adult life is when you grow up in poverty, the effects it can have on your life are about more than a just a lack of finances.

There are many distractions and challenges that can keep you from becoming and doing what God wants you to be and do. Ask yourself, "Am I living the life God wants me to live?" Take some time to reflect on that question. Allow the Holy Spirit to lead you to the truths about your current situation.

I remember when I started my self-assessment. My checking-in began after being a stay-at-home wife and mom for fourteen years. I remember waking up one day wondering who I was. Who had I become? Had I gotten lost on the journey? I had worked hard to get an education and was preparing for a career in the medical profession. I wanted to be a doctor, but I ended up being a wife and stay-at-home mother.

I had enjoyed taking care of our children, teaching and exposing them to all types of learning activities. I drove them to dance and music lessons, became their Girl Scout leader, and volunteered at their schools. I enrolled them in summer programs at the local university. I also stayed busy with my hobbies. However, I began to feel I was off-track. I had not carried out my plan A, and I didn't have an alternative one.

I got to a point in life where I began to look for *me*, not the wife to my husband, or the mother of our four children. What happened to the woman who worked hard to get an education so she could have a career? I believed I was blessed because there were not many black women in my circle who could stay home like me. This affected how I approached being a stay-at-home mom. I did so much to make staying home fit me that I overdid it. I thought I had to do everything perfectly. I didn't have role models to emulate.

One Christmas, I was so depressed that I had no interest in cooking for my family, nor going with them to other family members' homes to eat. What I was experiencing was beyond being blue or sad. I knew I had to do something to bring about change, but what? I had to figure out where I was on the journey, and who I had become. My plan "A" had been interrupted and I was feeling lost. It was self-examination time.

What I saw as a life interruption, Patricia Shirer calls a divine intervention. In her book, *Life Interrupted, Navigating the Unexpected,* she says, "We've all seen our Plan A's take a backseat to other realities – realities we just don't want to accept or live through. Yet, here they are. This is our life. We can run, but we can't hide."

Patricia Shirer suggests that when your first plan is not working, you must change your perspective. She says,

> What if we knew this interrupted life
> was less about the problem and more
> about the process? What if we knew
> this roadblock or aggravation hadn't
> caught God by surprise even if it comes
> as a shock to us? What if we knew that
> the direction He was taking us provided

opportunities we'd always dreamed about, even if they didn't look exactly how we thought they would? What if we knew, by not getting what we wanted, God was ultimately giving us something better?

Shirer uses the Biblical account of the Prophet Jonah and his call to go to Nineveh to demonstrate how what he saw as an interruption, was a divine intervention.

Another Biblical character we can learn from when our Plan A isn't working is Saul. Saul had an interruption in his life that turned out for his and our good. His divine intervention happened as he was on the road to Damascus to persecute Jews who were following the Way. These were Jews who had heard the Gospel and were now following Christ. Saul had obtained papers to arrest followers and bring them back to Jerusalem for punishment.

Saul's plan was changed on the Damascus road when he had an encounter with Christ. He fell to the ground and heard Christ speaking to him. Saul responded with, "What shall I do, Lord?" Jesus gave him a new plan to follow. Saul was blinded after the encounter, so his men had to lead him into Damascus where he met Ananias.

Paul gives the Jews an account of his conversion in Acts 22. He tells them his plan was to persecute Christians (his Plan A). However, Ananias gives him his Plan B, the opposite of what he started out to do. Ananias told him,

> The God of our fathers chose you long ago to know His plan. He chose you to see the Righteous One and to hear words from Him. You will be His witness to all people. You will tell them what you have witnessed and heard. Now, don't wait any longer. Get up, be baptized and wash away your sins, trusting in Jesus to save you. (Acts 22:14-15, ERV)

I want you to think about how much better Saul's Plan B (God's plan for him) was. He had a conversion experience like no other, a name change, and a commission from God that has impacted Christianity. Paul's ministry included planting churches, teaching, preaching, and writing much of the New Testament.

When I look back at my life and the interruption in my plan A, I now know it was more about the process, rather than the interruption. It was my plan for my life and not God's. I needed God to intervene in my life and give me His plan. God's intervention was for me to learn who I was and who

He wanted me to become. His plan was so much better for me, even if I didn't recognize it at the time.

If you believe you're not where you're supposed to be or your current plan is not working in your best interest, it's time for an assessment. You may have made your Plan A without consulting God, or made it at a time when you didn't have accurate information or resources. Like me, you may not have really known who you were at the time you made your Plan A. Whatever the reason, please consider doing an assessment now.

This examination is not to be a mental one. It is to be a soul searching one that engages the Holy Spirit in guiding you through the process. It's one where you allow yourself to be transparent as you truly look at every area of your life – social, spiritual, emotional, mental and financial.

These areas of your life are interconnected, so if you're experiencing difficulty in one area, it can wreak havoc in another one. If you're having repeated negative thoughts (mental), it can affect how you interact with others (social), your relationship with God (spiritual), how you see yourself (emotional), and how you make decisions about how to spend money (financial).

I thought I would be blown away by all my "stuff" when I began my assessment process many years ago. I had been carrying around tons of baggage from the past. Yet, I was at a place that the Holy Spirit was urging me, saying, "It's time to unload."

Early in the process, I realized I was at yet another juncture where I didn't know where or to whom to turn. Although I had grown up in a religious home, I was not spiritually mature. I didn't know I could ask the Holy Spirit to guide and teach me concerning all things. However, there was a knowing that God would reveal my heart to me as I allowed myself to be open to Him.

Remember, this is the checking-in phase of the process. You're not trying to fix what's broken in your life; not now. Keeping this in mind will give you the freedom to be open during the process. Knowing that my God had intimate knowledge of me helped me be transparent in this process. He made me and knows my purpose.

A good way to begin your self-examination is with this knowledge, "You are an awesome wonder whom God created to be here to carry out His purpose for you in the earth."

Develop a list of positive statements you can read over and over to give you the courage to persevere through the fear and whatever else would block your progress in this assessment. Remember God is in the midst of your situation, showering you with His peace, love, and joy.

Knowing God loves you unconditionally can also help you with your, "Where am I?" examination.

And because He loves you, He doesn't want to leave you where you are if it's not in keeping with His plan for your life. You are fearfully and wonderfully made, so see yourself that way. Garner up the courage and begin the process. You are so worth it. Consider getting professional help if you find this process too difficult for you to do alone.

Accepting you as you are and for where you are is so important to the examination process. I had to learn this in order to move from a place of pain to one of peace and joy. The transforming power of God is with you every step of the way. You must believe this so you can displace the lies of the enemy that say you are okay where you are and there is no need for you to change. Make a decision to allow your Creator to tell you what changes are needed.

God has intimate knowledge of you. Allow Him to jumpstart your identity journey. God will show you the areas you need to examine and change to get to your truest identity.

IT'S YOUR TURN

Remember, you're doing this exercise to determine where you are in life, not to condemn yourself for being there. You may find that you're exactly where God wants you to be. If not, it's still okay to discover where you are presently. Remember, YOU ARE AN AWESOME WONDER.

Sit quietly with soaking music.*   Say a prayer asking the Holy Spirit to be with you during the exercise, and give you discernment. End the exercise with a prayer of thanks.

Exercise: Look in the mirror and ask seven times, "Where am I?"

Wait a few minutes for the answers to come. Write your answers in the space provided on the next page. Now, write down where you want to be. Are there differences? You will have the opportunity later in the book to identify what internal and external obstacles contributed to you being where you are and what to do about it so you can make movement.

---

*Soaking Music, also known as Soaking Prayer and Soaking Worship music is Christian music used during prayer and reflection. Listening to Soaking Music can enable you to set aside self and focus and meditate on God for renewal of strength and peace (Wikipedia, the free encyclopedia).

MY ASSESSMENT

Where are you in life now?	Where had you expected to be by now?

IT'S YOUR TURN

Five Area Assessment

In this assessment, I want you to examine how you're doing financially, spiritually, socially, emotionally, and mentally. Write a statement about where you are presently in each area. Then write where you want to be in the future. For example, in the financial area, I'm $5,000 in debt. Is there where you want to be? If not, what do you want? Do you want to decrease your debt or be debt free in the future? Write your desires for the future.

If you find this assignment difficult to complete, do not stress. You can always come back to this assignment. As you continue to read further in the book, the Holy Spirit may lead you back here and the answers will just flow.

Financial:
Presently:

_____

_____

Future:

_____

_____

Spiritual:

Presently:

_____

_____

Future:

_____

_____

Emotional:

Presently:

_____

_____

Future:

_____

_____

Social:

Presently:

_____

_____

Future:

_____

_____

Mental:
Presently:

_____

_____

Future:

_____

_____

WHAT DO I DO NOW?

Now that you've assessed the different areas of your life, I want you to write about the differences you discovered between where you are now and where you thought you'd be. Do this exercise in a free-write style. In free write, you put your pencil to paper and just write (make sure you have extra sheets of paper on hand or use your journal for this exercise).

Don't be concerned about spelling, punctuation, or grammar. Just write what comes freely. I'm starting you off with a prompt. You may want to consider writing about who, what, when, where, and how. For example, who did you allow to get you off track? How did they do it? When did it happen? etc.

I'm at this place in my life because:

_____

_____

_____

_____

_____

_____

Forget the former things; do not dwell on the past.

Isaiah 43:18 (NIV)

Brethren, I do not count myself to have apprehended; but one thing I do, forgetting those things which are behind and reaching forward to those things which are ahead, I press toward the goal for the prize of the upward call of God in Christ Jesus.

Philippians 3:13-14 (NKJV)

CHAPTER 3

Leaving the Past Behind

You have been shaped by your past, but you don't have to be defined by it. You don't have to allow the past to rob you of peace and joy presently, or in your future. However, it becomes necessary for you to examine your past, especially if it was filled with trauma and betrayal. Sometimes it's necessary to look back in order to move forward.

I think of trauma as any negative event that causes a person pain in different areas of their life. This pain often continues over a long period of time. For example, childhood physical abuse is a trauma that negatively that affects emotional and mental health, even into adulthood. You usually develop some type of survival strategy to help you deal with traumas.

Looking back so you can move forward may sound a little strange. However, at some time, you must deal with the pains of the past and unload the baggage you've been carrying. Just imagine you have a suitcase and every time you experience pain, you stuff it in the suitcase and keep going.

Examining your past and living in the past are entirely different. The mistake one sometimes make is sometimes made is getting stuck in the past. What is needed is the identification of the traumas in your past and their effect on your present and future.

What I found as I examined my past was I had developed all types of survival skills to survive in my environment. Using these survival strategies didn't rid me of my pain, they just allowed me to suppress it. I really thought the pain was buried until it kept showing up in my daily life. I realized a healthy approach was needed to deal with the pain.

One may believe living with and suppressing pain is how life is supposed to be. Have you heard a person say, "I have no control over my circumstances; I have to live like this." This is a lie from the enemy that has become this person's truth.

Moving beyond this thinking requires one to refute lies, change thinking, and identify the traumas and resolve them. This is no easy task. I realized it takes giant-sized courage to deal with the past in preparation to move on to destiny.

I had a very interesting and painful past I needed to leave behind so I could live in the present and prepare for the future. I had a history of childhood abuse that was hard for me to shake, no matter how hard I tried. At one time, I had the idea that the past would always be in my present, preventing me from becoming the person God designed me to be.

When I attempted to talk to family or friends about my past, I heard statements coming from well-meaning people that were not helpful like, "Girl you need to leave the past behind you. You need to stop looking back and remembering the bad things that happened to you when you were a child. I don't know why you allow that stuff from your past to bother you now; it happened such a long, long time ago."

They were trying to help the best way they knew how. They were telling me to get on with life without working through the pains of the past. I realized they were telling me to do what they did when they were hurt. It just didn't feel right to me.

I believe not looking back, not thinking about the pain, and/or not remembering is NOT the answer to getting over pains of the past. I realized I needed more if I was going to make peace with my past. I understood I needed to leave the past behind because it was all up in my present life causing problems.

I knew I needed professional help. However, seeing a therapist was taboo in my family and community. I made the decision to do whatever it took to save me. I summoned the courage to get professional help so I could get myself prepared for the more God had in store for me. That meant learning who I had become, how far I was off the path God had set for me, and what I had to do to get back on track.

In the first session with the therapist, as he began to ask me questions about different phases of my life, the pains of the past began to come to the surface.

As I sat there holding back tears, he looked at

me and said, "You're talking about some painful experiences. Don't you feel like crying?"

Just as I started to answer no, the tears came streaming down. The dam I had been using to hold the tears broke. I cried and cried. The more I cried, the more the therapist encouraged me to cry.

He told me, "You've been holding on to pain for such a long time that you've become afraid to allow yourself to deal with it. You've also stopped yourself from crying when you're hurting. I want you to allow yourself to cry. If you start to cry while driving home today, drive to a safe place, park your car and cry. You'll be okay. It will be cleansing."

Of course, while driving home, I began to cry. I pulled to a safe place and let the tears roll down. It wasn't just tears; there were gut wrenching sobs. I don't know how long I cried. What I do know is something happened as a result of the crying. I released a lot of pain that had been tightly stored in the cells of my body, causing problems. The frozen part of me had tried not to feel because of the weight of the pain. I actually felt lighter when I arrived home.

The therapist wanted to know what had caused me to shut down and not cry. I had been a very sensitive child who cried a lot. I had sandy red hair and reddish skin growing up. On top of that, I have a large nose. I got teased a lot, so I cried a lot.

I also cried when I got beatings, not from the beatings, but from the harsh words spoken while I was being beaten. Teaching myself to shut down and not cry helped me to survive in my environment. Not crying meant I was not weak and vulnerable. That's the lie I learned to believe. I realized it was one of my survival strategies developed during childhood.

When you're a child, survival strategies can be protective and helpful. They are the things you teach yourself to do so you feel safe. You may find that you developed strategies just to survive in your environment during the checking-in process of your journey. These survival strategies were developed to help you cope with whatever traumas you faced. You'll need to ask and answer truthfully, "Are the survival skills working for me in adulthood?" They may have worked for you in childhood, but are inappropriate now.

I cried out to God to help me. I needed some resolution. Pains and wounds from the past are real and are often very hard to resolve. However, the past can be put behind you, where it can't touch or trouble you emotionally when you allow God to heal you.

The emotions attached to pains from the past can be resolved and rendered powerless over you. Trust me, I know. Today, I find it amazing how I can talk and write about my past without experiencing the emotions that were previously attached to it. I have dealt with those wounds that were holding me back.

We give the past, or should I say, the enemy, the power to keep us locked up and blocked by reliving the past, but not working through it. God allows us to absolve our past by giving us the strength to revisit and release the negative emotions attached to it.

Getting to the real you will require you to leave your past with all its baggage behind. Emotional baggage is heavy and can weigh you down. Graham Cooke says, "Baggage is made up of the hurts and pains you collect from your past." He suggests you drop the baggage by dealing with the past, and exchange it for luggage. God then fills the luggage you pick up with love, joy, peace, patience, kindness, goodness, faithfulness, gentleness, and self-control. (Galatians 5:22-23, ERV).

You can examine your current behaviors to determine the influence of the past upon them. If you are still responding to certain life situations as you did in childhood, it is a strong indication that you are locked in an old pattern. In the past, you developed these responses just so you could survive in your family. Children can end up broken if they live in a family where the adults can't or don't provide what's needed for them to grow up healthy and whole.

You must become aware of and own inappropriate behaviors and responses if you are to change them. This can be a difficult task because no one wants to admit they are stuck in the past and still responding to situations as they did when they were a child. To help with this awareness, consider the possible effects of past pains on your present behavior:

- You respond to situations in a childlike manner because old issues with parents are stirred up.
- You continue to hear mom or dad's disapproving voice in situations.
- You get in and stay in unhealthy relationships.
- You don't set goals because you fear failing; your parents said you wouldn't do anything worthwhile.
- You don't have good decision-making skills.
- You don't spend (even when you can afford to), or you overspend.
- You don't live up to your potential because of fear.
- You may speak to people in an angry or a childlike voice.
- You are guarded and do not express your feelings openly.
- You develop unrealistic expectations of people.
- You don't acknowledge or talk about problems for fear of upsetting things.
- You may put others first for fear that you will be called selfish.
- You don't know how to have fun.
- You communicate by sulking or acting out.

- You go along with family and friends' decisions because you fear rejection.
- You become quiet in an attempt to avoid bringing attention to yourself.

The above is not a complete listing of behaviors that result from growing up in a dysfunctional family. However, you can use it to begin looking at your current behaviors. If you are an adult child of an alcoholic, for example, you probably developed responses to keep yourself safe when your parent(s) drank. The behavior you undoubtedly learned was to be quiet in an attempt to not bring attention to yourself for fear that you would be beaten, shouted at, etc.

When I began my journey to healing, I had to identify and examine how I had dealt with the dysfunction in my family. I created a list of inappropriate behaviors which resulted from childhood survival strategies while working with a therapist. I set a goal of saying goodbye to them because they were no longer working and were not needed in my life (more about this when it's your turn).

I felt "different" from my family when I was growing up. They teased me a lot so I figured that if I became quiet and invisible, I would not be bothered. I got good at disappearing while still being present in a situation. That survival skill served me well in childhood. I believed that disappearing was helpful and protective.

Some survival skills you developed and used as a child were inappropriate. However, you continued to use them because they brought you security. It becomes difficult to develop new ways of being because you may not trust yourself to develop more appropriate coping skills. One of the long-term effects of trauma is the inability to trust yourself to learn what is appropriate and what is not, what is normal and what is not.

It's important to learn to recognize when your survival strategies have become counterproductive in your life. Once you recognize that the use of strategies from the past are a problem, it's time to do something; it's time to change. You need to garner the courage to take an honest look at your inner pain. It is time to remove the mask and feel the pain. Again, I suggest you seek professional help to guide you through this process, especially if you've experienced lots of traumas.

Remember, you can't change the past because the events have already taken place. If your parents were verbally, physically, and/or sexually abusive, there was really nothing you could've done about it as a small child. That child of your past still exists inside you, wounded. As an adult, you can change your present and prepare for the future by validating, healing, and integrating your inner child of the past.

Your inner child comes to earth naturally trustful, intuitive, and self-loving. Growing up in a family that doesn't provide proper nurturing can contaminate the child and cause her to develop a set of core beliefs that are not in keeping with who she really is. For me to survive in my environment, there were certain beliefs I adopted and lived by. I had no idea what "normal" was for a child, teen, or adult until I began my healing journey. I felt so messed up because of what happened to me as a child.

My parents told me what to do, and how to think when I was growing up. Truth be told, this continued even into young adulthood until I left home. According to my mother, I was a determined child with a mind of my own. This was not the type of child you wanted to be in my family. My mother didn't like that I wanted to think for myself. My natural wonder child turned into a wounded child that didn't know how to be in the family I was born into.

The inner child of my past, who was very sensitive, was so wounded that it has taken me years to recover her, nurture her, and integrate her into my being. Little Joyce (as I call her) was so present in my adult life, wanting expression. However, it was not in a way that was good for me. There are still times when I have to stop and say to the child within, "I've got this." Then, the adult me handles the situation in an appropriate manner.

It was in adulthood that I had to learn to truly trust myself. That was rather scary. I couldn't trust because I was constantly hurt by people's words and actions. The hurt was so strong, I questioned myself all the time. I questioned my actions constantly. I couldn't even believe or trust I was worth loving.

The survival strategies I developed in childhood helped me erect a wall of protection around my heart. This wall was built after each hurt or trauma, one brick at a time. When I started tearing down my wall, it was if I could identify what the brick was made of and what contributed to it being there. For example, the brick of "undeserving" was built when I was told I was no good and would never amount to anything. It fit into the low self-esteem brick. The bricks in my protective wall were reinforcing each other, making the wall stronger and stronger.

I built the wall during childhood when my identity was developing. It became a real operating part of me as I interacted with my environment. I believed it kept me safe. It became my stronghold. However, while doing healing work, I discovered that a wall built in a person's life can keep love out and hurt in. The walls must come down or they become strongholds in your life. I had to tear down the wall because it kept me from accepting who God said I was, and who He wanted to be for me.

Living in the past takes away energy that you need to live in the now. It's time to determine if you're allowing pains of the past to rob you. If they are, it's time to let them go. I understand this may be hard; it was for me. Can we agree that you won't give fear the power to prevent you from revisiting and letting go of past pains?

Going from here to there can be very freeing and exciting. In this process, you're disconnecting from pain and connecting to truths about you. You learn to trust the wisdom within. You may need to turn away from listening to what others may say about you. Begin listening to and learning to believe what God says about you.

There has been nothing in my life as wonderful as having children. I wanted to give them a life different from mine. I wanted them to especially feel loved. I had not been shown love growing up, so I didn't know how to demonstrate it. However, making peace with my past enabled me to love God, myself, and others – especially my children.

I was rewarded for doing journey work one day when I was loving on one of my children. She asked me how I knew how to love them – to give hugs and kisses. I believed she asked me this because I had told her about my childhood. With what she knew, she wondered how I was able to express love to her. God had worked a miracle in my life because I was willing to open up and get rid of the pain. Working through issues, and making peace with your past can work wonders in your life.

A necessary ending can produce a wonderful new beginning. As Graham Cooke says, "You want thinking and behavior to be present-future rather than present-past." That is, you don't want to allow your past to keep you living there (in the past). You want to live in the present so God can show you your future.

In the next two chapters, I share strategies I used to rid myself of baggage. The journey to the Truest You begins with unloading all the "stuff" that would hold you back. As you unpack pains of the past, you free up space that then can be filled with love, joy, peace, and a whole host of other wonderful things.

I believe that in preparation to move to destiny and purpose, there is a need to revisit the past, but not get stuck there. Saying goodbye to behaviors that no longer serve you well takes courage and time. You begin to see the real you when you stay the course and are successful in ending the past's power over you.

I was visiting a church where people dance up front during the music portion of praise and worship. There was a lady wearing a bright orange T-shirt with writing on it. She was dancing wildly, so it took me some time to read what was on her shirt. Once I could read what was on it, I understood why she was dancing as she was. It read: *I traded my stuff for His Joy.*

Ending that phase of your life, where the past influences your current behavior, is a necessity. You need to journey with as light a load as possible. God gives you grace to put the past in the past where it does not torment you anymore. However, you must be willing to go through the process, and then let the pain go. When you are willing to do this, look at what God promises. Isaiah 43:18-20, reads,

> So don't remember what happened in earlier times. Don't think about what happened a long time ago, because I am doing something new! Now you will grow like a new plant. Surely you know this is true. I will even make a road in the desert, and rivers will flow through that dry land. (ERV)

See yourself walking away from the influence of your past. Walk out of and into the present and plan for a prosperous future.

IT'S YOUR TURN

This exercise takes you back in time so you can determine when you started to leave your truest self and why. You may not be able to go all the way back. That's okay. Many individuals fear going back. They have become so accustomed to "stuffing" negative feelings when hurtful situations occur that they're afraid of what may happen to them if they just stop and deal with the issue. Like me, you may fear being overwhelmed by the rush of painful memories. Please don't allow this to prevent you from doing this exercise. I didn't.

Try to avoid the **"what if's"** as you begin this exercise. What if I start crying and can't stop? What if I can't control myself, etc.? I have done this exercise many times on my journey. I remember being afraid, yet going forward. I'm so happy I did because of the benefits. Ask Jesus to keep you safe if you fear going back.

This exercise for dealing with the past is one that I do in Inner Healing sessions with individuals. When I assigned this exercise for individuals to do at home, I would tell them to ask a friend to call them thirty minutes from the time they begin. This takes away the fear of crying and not being able to stop. Someone will be checking on you after thirty minutes. You also ask Jesus to allow His peace to keep you calm.

Remember, I also suggest that you consider getting professional help as you do the exercises if you become too afraid or discouraged.

Now, sit or lie down in a comfortable place. Playing instrumental soaking music may help you to relax. Now take several deep breaths: breathe in slowly (to the count of five) while pushing your stomach out, hold for a count of seven, then exhale slowly (to a count of nine) letting your stomach go in. Do this five times. You can do the deep breathing any time to keep fear abated. You can be in charge of the thoughts that cause any anxiety.

You have the power to take all negative thoughts captive. To encourage yourself, read 2 Corinthians 10:3-5 which reads,

> We live in this world, but we don't fight our battles in the same way the world does. The weapons we use are not human ones. Our weapons have power from God and can destroy the enemy's strong places. We destroy people's arguments, and we tear down every proud idea that raises itself against the knowledge of God. We also capture every thought and make it give up and obey Christ.

Now, think back to the first time you experienced trauma. Don't minimize any trauma you've experienced in the past. I've heard women talk about a traumatic experience, such as childhood physical abuse, then say, "Oh, it was nothing."

The negative feelings resulting from traumatic experiences may have become a part of you. You may not even recognize this. I want you to answer the following questions: What became your normal response to traumatic situations? When did that start? What was the situation that triggered your flight or fight response?

As you continue to breathe deeply, ask yourself to recount the lies you began to believe about what happened to you. Did you learn to believe you were worthless? Did you believe you had no control over what happens to you? Did you believe you were damaged from what happened to you? Did you feel responsible for what happened to you? What survival strategies did you learn in your past that affect your today?

Write down your discoveries in a journal or on the next page. Look at your discoveries and how they play out in your present. Have the negative thoughts and behaviors become a normal part of your life?

When I've done this exercise (many, many times), I made so many discoveries. I discovered I had low self-esteem, felt unworthy, and did not believe I could make decisions that were good for me. I also allowed guilt and shame to affect my behavior. As a result, I became shy. Outwardly, I became an overachiever to hide what I was feeling inside. I'll tell you more about changing these thought patterns in a later chapter. For now, I want you to look at your past and how it affects your present, and could possibly affect your future.

IT'S YOUR TURN

The Effect of the Past on my Present

What are the recurring negative thoughts from your past?	What negative behaviors resulted from those thoughts and show up in your present life?

After the exercise, listen to quiet music and read Scriptures. Highlight your favorite Scriptures and commit them to memory.

WHAT DO I DO NOW?

Now that you've completed the exercise, ask yourself, "What did I learn about myself, and are there things I want to change?" This exercise is very freeing because you have the opportunity to look at the lies you've believed, and now turn them into truths. Right now, I want you to choose one lie and the resulting behavior to write about. I'll start you off:

I learned to believe I was no good so I

_____

_____

_____

_____

_____

I now know the truth, so I'm changing (write about the behavior you stated above):

_____

_____

_____

_____

_____

_____

Now without my prompting, choose another lie and the resulting behavior:

_____

_____

_____

_____

_____

I now know the truth, so I'm changing (write about the behavior you stated above):

_____

_____

_____

_____

Don't be angry with each other, but forgive each other. If you feel someone has wronged you, forgive them. Forgive others because the Lord forgave you.

(Colossians 3:13, ERV)

Forgive us the wrongs we have done as we ourselves release forgiveness to those who have wronged us. "And when you pray, make sure you forgive the faults of others so that your Father in heaven will also forgive you. But if you withhold forgiveness from others, your Father withholds forgiveness from you."

Matthew 6:12, 14, and 15 (TPT)

CHAPTER 4

Forgiveness is Freedom

Forgiveness is a freeing process that can lead to inner healing. In the Greek, forgiveness means to send away the hurt, bitterness, and pain of an offense. It does not mean excusing, forgetting, or belittling the harm. Instead, it involves changing your mind about the person who has committed the wrongdoing, and saying "I forgive you." This doesn't have to be a face-to-face encounter.

Forgiveness may not be easy, but it is necessary for healthy living on your journey. It takes sincere and diligent practice over time to forgive. Pains and wounds from the past caused by someone's wrongdoings are real and sometimes very hard to resolve. The emotions attached to past traumas can be resolved and rendered powerless over you thorough forgiveness.

God forgives as only He can. He gave His only begotten Son to die for our sins, past, present and future. This was done to bring us back into a right relationship with Him. "If we confess our sins, He is faithful and just and will forgive us our sins and purify us from all unrighteousness." (1John 1:9, NIV) He not only forgives our sins, but God remembers them no more.

Just as God forgives us, He commands us to forgive others. According to Scriptures, you must forgive those who have offended you, forgive from the heart, receive forgiveness from God, and forgive yourself. The latter is sometimes the hardest to do.

If you forgive others for their transgressions, your heavenly Father will also forgive you. But if you do not forgive others, then God will not forgive your sins. The importance of forgiveness is included in the "model" prayer. In Matthew 6:9-13 we read, "Forgive us the wrongs we have done as we ourselves release forgiveness to those who have wronged us." (TPT)

Sherri Lewis suggests that choosing to forgive is a decision one makes. "Once you decide to forgive, the work begins." Forgiveness is a process – something that takes place over time. I believe that if you have been severely wounded, you may forgive a little at a time, so as not to be overwhelmed by the process. You also want to make sure that you are truly letting go of the offense.

Since forgiveness is a process, here are steps to take:

- Acknowledge that you have unforgiveness in your life.
- Ask the Holy Spirit to give you the ability to look at the full impact of the hurt on you.
- Make the decision to forgive.

- Allow the Holy Spirit to show you how to forgive and release the offender.
- Ask God to heal the wounds of the offense.
- Ask God to fill the empty space with His love.

A person needs the Holy Spirit, Jesus, and God at the beginning and throughout the forgiveness process because of the difficulty sometimes involved. The Holy Spirit enables you to discern the unforgiveness. Jesus is your companion during the process (see Him holding your hand). God's love is there to protect you, provide deliverance, and then tell you who you really are, once you let go.

Give yourself the gift of forgiveness, like I did. For so many years, I had believed forgiveness was what the person who had wronged you asked for. Boy, was I wrong in so many ways. I was more concerned about my fears and concerns than obeying the Word of God. I was afraid that if I forgave, it was giving approval to what the person had done.

I had been wronged and was carrying around and attempting to bury the pain as best as I could. My biggest desire was for my parents, who had hurt me, to acknowledge it, ask me to forgive them, and repent of the behaviors. Maybe you believe, like I did, that you have to hold on to the trauma until the offender did his or her part in the forgiveness process. That is a lie from the enemy. The truth is, the offender is going about their life while you are stuck with guilt and shame.

Another strategy the enemy uses is to make you feel responsible for the trauma you experienced. This can prevent you from holding a person responsible for what they did, thereby interfering with the forgiveness process. When you're thinking about the painful situation, you develop a list of things you could have done to prevent the maltreatment. The list may look something like this depending on the abuse:

- "What if I hadn't worn a red dress. Would I have been raped?
- "What if my body wasn't developing? Would he have sexually abused me?
- "What if I hadn't talked back to him? Would he have hit me?
- "What if I'd been a better wife? Would he have gone out and cheated on me?
- "What if I didn't act like my father. Would my mother love me?

In the above illustrations, the victim takes the responsibility for what happened to them. They believe if they had acted differently, the abuse would not have taken place. This further complicates the situation because if they feel responsible, they will not want to talk to anyone about the abuse. As a child I was traumatized by abuse and threats not to tell. There was no way I was going to tell, and then have people make me responsible for what happened.

The problem with the "what if" game is that it imprisons you. It sometimes forces you to respond with behaviors that are not in your best interest. For example, individuals believing the "what ifs" listed above may respond with the following behaviors and thoughts:

- **Behavior**: A woman will stop wearing her favorite color red.
  Thought: She thinks it's too provocative.

- **Behavior:** The young girl dresses to hide her developing body.
  Thought: She thinks she's responsible for the sexual abuse because her body changed from that of a little girl.

- **Behavior:** The wife becomes quiet.
  Thought: She thinks her talking caused him to hit her.

- **Behavior:** The wife works harder and harder in the marriage.
  Thought: She thinks if she does more, he will be pleased with her and stay home.

- **Behavior:** The boy works to change his behavior so he's not like his father.

    Thought: He thinks that he can make his mother treat him nice if he's not like his father (although he does not know his father).

Much unforgiveness results from maltreatment during childhood. Childhood traumas include neglect, physical abuse, emotional abuse, and sexual abuse. George A. Boyd states,

> When you grow up in a dysfunctional family, you experience trauma and pain from your parents' actions, words, and attitudes. Because of this trauma you experienced, you grew up changed, different from other children, missing important parts of necessary parenting that prepare you for adulthood, missing parts of your childhood when you were forced into unnatural roles within your family.

Guilt and shame are two pervasive emotions that result from traumas, especially with children. These emotions often make forgiveness difficult. It is so important to recognize there is a difference between the two if you are to heal. You experience guilt when you believe you've done something bad. Shame makes you believe that you *are* bad as the result of something someone has done to you.

The shame resulting from childhood traumas affect your thinking, mood, actions, and behavior. All this affects your sense of self. I felt deeply wounded because of the shame I carried with me daily. There was no escaping it. I even became an "overachiever" to compensate for the negative feelings I experienced. Gershen Kaufman says, "Shame is the most disturbing experience individuals ever have about themselves; no other emotion feels more deeply disturbing because in the moment of shame the self feels wounded from within."

The all-encompassing shame you feel after you've experienced mistreatment can take you further off course when you continue to carry it around. This is especially true for individuals who were sexually abused. When the abuse has taken place in childhood and the child is unable to tell because of a threat, they may carry the pain for a lifetime, making forgiveness even harder.

Sexual abuse can be any physical contact between an adult and child where that contact must be kept secret and it violates the child. The assaults, which can range from genital exposure to intercourse, and the effects are devastating and can last a lifetime if victim does not seek professional help.

I wanted to include information on some issues survivors deal with. I hope this information will help you if you have been abused and haven't dealt with the trauma. I trust you will be encouraged to get help.

I'm sorry you were abused; you didn't deserve that horrific treatment. If you were sexually abused as a child and haven't received professional counseling, you may still be carrying around shame and guilt which can show up in self-destructive behaviors.

What can make sexual assault devastating is when the abuser is a close relative. In my case, my father abused me. The molestation took place over many years. To this day, I don't remember when it started or ended. I believe I was a little girl, around seven or eight. This lack of memory around traumas is not unusual. It's a protective factor so you can keep functioning.

The molestation affected me in so many areas. I grew up with feelings of guilt and shame, low self-esteem, mistrust, confusion, misunderstandings about love and sex, and so much more. I have had to learn to trust, not just people, but God, Jesus and the Holy Spirit. My father was a pastor. His role as a father was to protect me, provide for me, and give me my identity. This, he did not do. Instead, he took away my innocence.

I believe the potential lifelong effects of childhood sexual abuse can be attributed to the lies one learns to embrace about themselves and the perpetrator, and the energy it takes to keep it a secret. I was a victim, yet I believed I caused the abuse. I thought it was my fault and I should've been able to make it stop. Oh, the magical thinking of a child. The child believes they can have power over a given situation, and takes on responsibility for the other person's behavior.

The earlier the abuse begins, the more detrimental it can be. As a child, I was constantly trying to figure out why my father was abusing me. Because the person abusing me was a close relative, my child's mind wanted to understand why my father was hurting me, rather than loving me and doing the right things fathers do. Like most sexually abused children, I was too frightened of the consequences to risk telling another adult what was happening.

You do what you can at that age to make the abuse stop. For example, I would sleep in pants (sometimes two pair), sleep in the middle of two sisters, and sleep at the head, rather than at the foot of the bed where I was more accessible. I worked hard not to be alone with him, sit next to him, or be told to rub his back. I did what I could to make myself inaccessible. Most of the time it didn't work. After all, he was the father and I was his child. He was in charge and told me what to do.

The threats used by my father created such fear in me. My father threatened to kill me with a gun if I told anyone. The threats of him killing me were as real as the beatings I got. He had a shotgun he kept in the house. He would take the gun down periodically to clean and show. The possibility of being killed by an abusive father was real to my young mind. Who was I going to tell anyway? I endured the molestation until I was no longer in the age range my father liked. I later learned that pedophiles, adults who abuse children, prefer children in a certain age range, so that's probably why he began to leave me alone.

As I mentioned earlier, my father was a pastor. I saw him as God's earthly representative. I began to question God. How could He allow my father to do what he did at home during the week and get in the pulpit and preach on Sunday? I began to blame God because in my child's mind, I thought God could and should've prevented the molestation.

Later, I had to accept that God gives us choices, and my father, not God, chose to molest me. I also had to accept that my father was a misrepresentation of what a loving father was.

The guilt and shame, and the feelings associated with the abuse took deep roots in my being. I worked with a therapist over a period of time to forgive my father, let go of inappropriate survival strategies I'd developed as a child, attempted to learn what was normal, and put new learning into daily practice.

Early in my adult life, I didn't recognize ways shame showed up in my life. In therapy, I learned how it had affected my development and thinking. Understanding what one thinks caused the shame and the related thoughts can cause varied expressions. Some ways shame was expressed in my life were:

- I became shy
- I was easily discouraged
- I was self-conscious
- I had feelings of inferiority

When you grow up in a family where no clear boundaries are set, it can lead to a variety of problems as you grow up. These problems can lead to depression, anxiety, alcoholism, drug abuse, eating disorders, sexual promiscuity, and other addictive behaviors. I am thankful to God I am only affected by two items from the list: depression and an eating disorder that shows up in overeating. I have been treated for the depression, and am learning to eat healthy.

Neglect was also present in my family. The children in my family had unmet needs that were revealed publicly. I remember how poorly we dressed as children and how embarrassing it was. It seemed as if everyone made fun of the way the Kelly children dressed. We accepted hand-me-downs from anyone, and wore the clothes given us, whether they fit or not. A pair of women's high-heeled shoes became shoes for a child once the heels were cut off. Of course, we got teased when the toes of the shoes turned up. We also wore shoes filled with paper to cover the holes, or no shoes at all in the summer.

When my siblings and I get together and talk about our past, we still remember how we dressed and how people talked about us. It still amazes me how not having decent clothes and shoes still plays a role not only in my life, but in the life of my siblings. You guessed it, we all have closets full of clothes and shoes. It's as if we made a conscious decision to not give people a reason to talk about how we dressed, ever again.

I went to school some days with no lunch or lunch money. We were lucky if we were chosen to work in the "lunchroom." If not, we stood in a line at the lunchroom back door and got a palm full of peanut butter for lunch. I remember thinking how nice Mrs. Adams was to feed us commodity peanut butter. To this day, I can still see myself trying to eat a handful of thick, dry peanut butter with no bread, no jelly, or water. At least I had some protein to sustain me through the day.

As you can see, I had many family issues to work through as I began my journey to my truest identity. At some point, I wanted to let go of unforgiveness in my life. Forgiveness can be difficult, especially if you're waiting for someone to ask for it. You can't get to your truest identity if you don't forgive. Remember forgiveness is for you. It is a gift of freedom.

I had struggled with my past and unforgiveness for years, and I do mean years. I now know it has affected every area of my life, especially spiritually, socially, and physically. I had to ask God for forgiveness for disobeying His word to forgive, repent of my unforgiveness behavior, and forgive my father and mother. This was hard for me, but I had to do it for my present and future. I needed to be free.

I began forgiving my father during traditional therapy sessions, and later continued in Sozo sessions. This was so difficult. I had to talk about his inappropriate behaviors, their effect on me, and then forgive him. The process included letting go of the responsibility I felt for the abuse as a little girl.

I remember someone telling me that God allowed me to do journey work so that I could help others with similar experiences as mine. Although the healing was for me, it was not just for me only. Doing journey work has prepared me to help others because I forgave and healed from my past's traumas. I share with you strategies I've used to deal with unforgiveness along my journey to my truest identity.

IT'S YOUR TURN

Are you ready to forgive? You may need to get professional help to deal with unforgiveness. I have worked with people who say they have forgiven someone, only to find they hadn't. When I've conducted sozos and the person tells me about an unhealthy relationship with their parents, I ask if they want to forgive them. They may say, "I have forgiven them already." During the session, I will usually suggest they ask the Holy Spirit if they need to forgive their parents. They are usually surprised at the unforgiveness they have been holding on to.

Make a list of people you need to forgive. You can ask the Holy Spirit to help you identify persons you have been "holding hostage" through unforgiveness. You may be surprised at the names that come up and their committed offense. I believe there will be a wide range of offenses. When I do the forgiveness exercise myself, I sometimes find myself saying, "You mean I've been holding on to that offense?"

Feel the freedom that comes from writing down the person's name, the offense, and then allowing the Holy Spirit to give you the strength to forgive and let go. You will probably begin to do a lot of deep releasing breaths here. I want you to watch how the self-discovery and self-reclaiming process begins when you forgive.

Forgiveness Worksheet

Are you ready to forgive and free yourself? Please remember you're doing this for you. Ask the Holy Spirit to help you identify the ones you need to forgive.

Person to forgive	Offense

For each person and offense, say, "I forgive you <u>(say their name)</u> for <u>(state the offenses)</u>. The person does not have to be present for you to forgive. Say it aloud and from your heart.

Forgiving Yourself

It's time to forgive yourself, now that you've forgiven others. Some believe this process is harder than forgiving others. Think back to how freeing it was when you forgave others. Well, this is going to be even better. It's time to stop beating yourself up over things you've done in the past that were not right. God has forgiven you if you asked. He wants you free.

Simply list the wrongs you've done, ask God to forgive you, then say, "I forgive me." Accept God's forgiveness.

1. _____

2. _____

3. _____

4. _____

5. _____

6. _____

7. _____

8. _____

9. _____

WHAT DO I DO NOW?

Now that you've forgiven, I want you to write about how you felt when you forgave yourself and others. Did you feel lighter? Did you breathe deep sighs of relief? What gifts did God give you to fill the empty places created by the forgiveness? Go deep as you complete this exercise. You can always add to this exercise as you go.

_____

_____

_____

_____

_____

_____

_____

_____

_____

_____

"Good people might have many problems, but the Lord will take them all away."

Psalm 34:19 (ERV)

"Remember, I commanded you to be strong and brave. Don't be afraid, because the Lord your God will be with you wherever you go."

Joshua 1:9 (ERV)

CHAPTER 5

Obstacles To Overcome

I had a row of Leland Cypress trees planted across the back of our yard soon after we moved into our new home in 2001. Eighteen years later, the trees have grown, but not all at the same rate. The ones on the end are about forty-five feet tall, while the ones in the center are only about fifteen feet tall. The growth of the shorter trees has been stunted by the tall trees in the lot behind our house. They keep them from getting much needed sun. The ones on the end are not growing in the shadow of the tall trees. The trees looming large (from the lot behind us) are an obstacle to the short Leland Cypress trees.

So it is in life. If you're in the shadow of something or someone, it can be an obstacle which prevents you from thriving. Having lived in these United States for over seventy-six years as a Black woman has taught me that you will have obstacles. What you must learn is what obstacles (I also call them "hoops" people expect you to jump through) are in your path, and how to deal with them. Journey obstacles can come from family, friends, and institutions.

According to Bessie Nchenge, Director, Bethel Atlanta Africa Transformation Center,

Obstacles block, hinder, or prevent your progress towards a goal. Obstacles are usually responsible for the gap between where you are and where you want to go. They are those frightful things you see when you take your eyes off your goals. You must step back and do an assessment to identify the obstacles in your life: what fuels your energy, what drains your energy, what things encourage you, and what are the discouragements in your life. Once you identify the obstacles, you begin the process of managing or removing them.

Obstacles can be both internal and external. Internal obstacles are factors within you that prevent you from reaching your goals (the negatives on the inside of you). For example, if a person has low self-esteem, it can prevent her from setting goals. The beliefs that result from low self-esteem are rooted in lies the person has learned to believe about themselves. Because they don't believe they can achieve, they don't even see setting goals as an option.

External obstacles are negative factors outside an individual that challenge their ability to reach a goal or fulfill a dream. External obstacles resulting from governmental systems, religion, culture, and family, are often beyond an individual's control. However, one can learn to manage the negative effects of them. One can usually learn to gain control over internal obstacles easier than external ones.

One thing I suggest you learn on your journey is which obstacles could pull you off your path, which ones you can ignore, and which ones you must take on. You can't fight every obstacle placed before you. I had to learn the Holy Spirit would help me discern which ones I was to take on and which ones I would allow God to fight.

As mentioned earlier, I was born and grew up in an impoverished area. From there, I moved to the suburbs in adulthood. I have also lived in eight different states, survived having a deadly blood clot in my lungs, raised four children in a racist environment, graduated from predominately white institutions (one was very prestigious), was elected and served on the Little Rock School Board during a tumultuous period, traveled the world, and have had many interesting careers.

Believe me, I can tell you a thing or two about journey obstacles – those things meant to take you off track. I want to share other obstacles I've faced on my journey and how I've dealt with them. I also include the obstacles of women I've worked with over the years. I share quotes from them, hoping you can identify with their struggles. It's easier to cope if you recognize you're not going it alone.

In overcoming both internal and external obstacles, you must discover when you started to believe the enemy's lies about them and their power over you. My experience has been, once I believed something about the obstacle's influence, there were systems set in place to reinforce those beliefs. For example, believing I was undeserving has had a tremendous impact on my life. I was led to believe I was not deserving of pretty much everything in my early adult years.

The lies coming from the external factors have a way of looking like truths. The educational system of my day held that a Black person was not deserving of equal access to education. My parents and their lack of support for me getting an education reinforced the educational system's lie that I didn't deserve a good education. The lies of these systems take on a life of their own. Living out these lies becomes your normal until you stop to examine the foolishness created by them. These lies can influence how you see yourself, and what you can or can't do.

Identifying, examining, and refuting the lies associated with obstacles is a process that takes place over time. To get to where I am today has taken a lot of overcoming power. Early in life, I believed there was no one there for me, so I had to go it alone. The lies that developed from those beliefs caused me to develop as a "Strong Black Woman," who could go it alone. That was a lie from the enemy, and I allowed it to become my truth and my normal. That is one lie

I've learned to refute and overcome on my journey. Well, most of the time.

The "Strong Black Woman" is one of those historical stereotypes that many of us have believed and allowed it to wreak havoc in our lives. Believing this label makes Black Women work harder and believe we can do it all. When we wear it, we feel like Superwomen. It doesn't allow for any weaknesses.

Read what Barbara, a fifty-something caseworker, said about an experience where she felt that she had to be strong, even though she was going through a heartbreaking situation.

> "I was at work and got a call from the police. They said that my son had been arrested for armed robbery. I could not believe what I was hearing. I talked to my supervisor and told him what was going on and got permission to leave work. I went to the police station to get additional information. He was arrested and was not being released on bail. When I finished at the police station, I went back to work. I didn't want them to think I was weak. I acted as if I was okay."

When asked about this be strong belief, she said, "That's what I was taught." She also said that different experiences in her work environment, family, church, and relationships had reinforced the belief that she had to be strong.

One of the many things I learned from my family when I was a stay-at-home mother and wife was I taught my family I was Superwoman, cousin to the Strong Black woman. I did just about everything for them. For example, when I did the laundry, I washed, folded, and put their clothes up. This was at a time when they were all capable of pitching in and sharing in family chores.

Being a perfect housewife had a harmful effect on me because I had become someone I didn't recognize. My sense of well-being was gone. Taking care of my family the way I did was my doing initially. My family enjoyed being taken care of so much, they were more than happy to support my being Superwoman. I didn't have anyone to show me how to take care of my family with balance. It was up to me to bring about change. My family wasn't about to give up what they were enjoying.

One day, I had a ceremony with my family and took off my Superwoman label. I actually made a label that had Superwoman on it and placed it on my forehead. As I was taking the label off, I told them I was going to be different – Suzy Homemaker, Superwoman, and Strong Black Woman were gone. I outlined to them what my expectations were and asked for feedback from them. I wanted my family to support me in the changes I needed to make.

Changing was not easy for me. My family didn't want to give up everything I had been doing for them. My next step was to go on strike. I just stopped doing certain things when they would not honor my request for help. When they decided to not put up the clothes I had washed and folded, I stopped washing.

I had a friend coming for a visit from Boston during my strike. My family was somehow convinced I would not have overflowing hampers with her coming, especially since my friend would be using the bathroom with the most overflow. Boy, they were mistaken. I told her about my strike and what to expect at the house when I picked her up at the airport. She congratulated me on the change I was making. We had a great visit, even with the overflowing hampers.

I believe fear is the biggest reason we continue to wear the "Strong Black Woman" label. We fear that if we are not there for everyone, and doing everything, people will leave us. When was the last time you stopped and asked yourself, "Why do I do all the things I do, and why do I operate with an overflowing plate?" You may find fear is mixed in there somewhere.

Black women are so accustomed to taking care of everyone but themselves. I have to ask, "How's that working for you?" I have to stop periodically and examine where I am and what I am doing. Are the things I'm doing in my best interest? Have I overstepped the boundary I have placed around me? Have I allowed someone to disrespect my limits? Asking and answering these questions have helped me "stay in my lane."

How we see ourselves – our self-image – can be another obstacle in our lives. Your self-image is developed from interaction and experiences with others. You learn about yourself from these experiences and societal influences. This can form the foundation of your belief systems and how you see you. Think about how you see yourself, and the things you say to and about you. The labels you place on yourself are the result of your self-image.

A person can have either a healthy self-image or an unhealthy one. When you have a healthy self-image, it is based on your thoughts, feelings, and perspective. You are no longer influenced by other people's opinion of you or by societal expectations. People with a positive self-image usually live a healthy lifestyle.

An unhealthy self-image can be damaging to one's well-being and how one functions in life. The unhealthy self-image usually results from negative perceptions one receives from their family, teachers, and other with whom they interact. It can prevent one from seeing their qualities and abilities. A person with an unhealthy self-image tends to focus on their limitations and flaws, rather than their positive traits. They are heavily influenced by external factors.

There are times when internal and external factors merge and result in tremendous negative effects on Black women. This can happen if one has low self-esteem (internal) and you believe society's definition of beauty (external). If you believe your skin is too dark for you to be beautiful, you may resort to using a bleaching cream to lighten your skin.

Let's now look at Black women and our tendency to not accept help from others. In addition to the take-care-of-everyone behavior, black women also refuse to accept help. We say yes when others ask for help, from loaning money (that doesn't get paid back in many instances), providing free housing, feeding, etc. However, we usually say no to offers of help from family and friends. It's as if you get a prized medal for not accepting help. We need to learn to say yes when help is offered and needed.

For many reasons, Black women become agents for everyone but themselves. We get so busy taking care of others, there's no time left for self-care. In my case, I believed the lie that I had to take care of others at my own expense. I was considered selfish if I didn't serve others. This belief was bolstered by my church's teaching on what was expected from a Christian. You were to be the helper, not the receiver. I now know it's self-love to take care of you – it's not selfish.

We don't begin to understand what dealing with the many obstacles in our lives costs us physically, spiritually, economically, and emotionally. For example, while teaching at a predominately white institution, I got sick my third year. What began as a sinus infection in September, progressed to bronchitis. It was not until May that I began to get better. I continued to teach, administer my grant, and do committee work. I later realized the stress of the job was contributing to my illness.

Another obstacle Black women must overcome is taking on false responsibility. I asked Carmen, a sixty-something single parent, to give me her view on false responsibility. She told me she would have to think about it and get back to me. Later she called and said, "I don't like you." In examining her thoughts about false responsibility, she didn't like what she had discovered. This is what she wrote:

> False, not actual. Responsibility—duty to deal with, having control over someone, accountable for. False responsibility is a big part of my life. Why? Robin Williams said, "I think the saddest people always try their hardest to make people happy because they know what it's like to feel absolutely worthless and they don't want anyone else to feel like that." I feel like you Robin. We take it upon ourselves to take the problems of others into our hands and try to make it better for them. Not because they ask us to, but because we

want to keep them from any hurt, harm, or danger. My children and grandchildren are my worst enemies. Why are they my enemies? Because I hold them in my heart too much. They don't ask me to keep them away from what is in my mind, "any hurt," but I do because of false responsibility. I found out that false responsibility can get you in trouble. What types of troubles you ask—money trouble, time trouble, sleep trouble, etc.

I also got a similar response from twenty-something Maxie, a single parent of two, when I asked her to tell me about her experience with false responsibility. She told me thinking about false responsibility had made her really think about other issues in her life. This is what she shared:

> My experience with false responsibility stemmed from a void I've been trying to fill much of my whole life. It blossomed into a lifestyle. Since I had convinced myself that I didn't deserve to be happy, I did everything in my power to be that hero that was always available and willing to lay down my life to see someone happy. Since I didn't have the luxury of support with raising my kids, I prided myself on helping siblings who had not reached a level of maturity in their parenting styles. So I assumed full responsibility because

I had the ability. I felt obligated and assumed that this was for a bigger cause. I felt it as a way to show the love that God had mirrored to me. As a result, I am currently a full-time baby sister on weekdays while working ten hour nights on weekends. In an effort to ensure that my four nieces and nephews don't fall victim to generational curses, I take on false responsibility.

What I found interesting about what the two women wrote above is they didn't ask me, nor did I offer an explanation of what false responsibility meant. There was no discussion of what I wanted them to include when they wrote. I believe that black women are very familiar with and are adept at taking on false responsibility.

For me, false responsibility is something I've taken on for a long time without even thinking about it, or planning to do it. False responsibility is something we believe we must take on and take care of, even though we don't have the authority or the ownership in the given situation. You do for others what they should do for themselves. During a therapy session, I recognized I started taking on responsibility for others as a child.

It's difficult to do nothing when you see something needs to be done, especially when you believe you have the answers. I had to learn not to take on false responsibility because it was burdensome. I learned I had stepped over the line and was operating in God's territory. When you rescue people, it prevents them from learning life lessons and moving into what God wants for them. God wants individuals to depend on *Him*, not you.

I remember when I was working with a black female therapist and she asked me if I was a little J.C. I asked, "a little J.C?" I had been telling her about something I had taken on that didn't belong to me. It was very clear I was trying to save the person. That why she asked if I was a little J.C. – Jesus Christ. Taking on false responsibility is one area in my life where I've had to constantly keep check on to make sure I wasn't slipping back into a behavior that at one time was my normal.

Another obstacle many Black women face which interferes with them having a decent quality of life is poverty. Poverty is multifaceted. It is the state of being poor, being in want or lack. It is the lack of enough money to provide for basic needs, opportunity, equality, and social support. When you look at poverty rates in the United States, they are highest among all Black family types when compared with all other US families. A part of this can be explained by the large number of Black women in low-paying service jobs, and the discrepancy in pay for Black women. For example, Black women make sixty-three cents ($.63) for every dollar ($1.00) earned by a white male.

I believe it's time for Black women to identify internal and external obstacles and the impact on their lives. Your journey work can be greatly impeded without you doing so. You can find yourself stuck and not able to move to the next level, yet not able to identify what's happening. My guess would be there are obstacles in your path you've not recognized or deemed creditable.

IT'S YOUR TURN

Identify obstacles in your life that have prevented you from being your truest self. What are those things you've allowed to take you off course, both internal and external? See if you can identify when this happened. Are there some things you can do to rid yourself of the obstacles?

Obstacle Internal or external	When did it come into your life?	What can you do to get rid of it?

WHAT DO I DO NOW?

This exercise requires you to draw. I want you to envision a road that will take you to your Truest identity. Now draw a two-lane road from one side of the paper to the other. On the left end of the road write, "I am here." At the right end of the road write, "My Truest identity." Now draw obstacles you think will be in your way as you journey, both internal and external ones. You can also cut out and use pictures from magazines. Put obstacles on both sides of the road.

What you should have is a picture of what you expect on your journey. I had you draw a two-lane road so you can move to a different lane if you want to avoid an obstacle. You also have the option to stop and deal with the obstacle. You choose. What you want is to get to your Truest identity.

Don't change yourselves to be like the people of the world, but let God change you inside with a new way of thinking. Then you will be able to understand and accept what God wants for you. You will be able to know what is good and pleasing to Him and what is perfect.

Romans 12:2 (ERV)

CHAPTER 6

INNER HEALING

Daryl Coley recorded a song entitled "Removal of the Mask." He sings about a person who publicly appeared to be whole. The person was hiding behind a mask. However, upon removing the mask, the person was not whole, but was fragmented, broken, and in bondage. This masked person wanted to be free – free of facades.

This song describes the process to become free from pain and the need to wear masks. The first step was the recognition that something had happened to cause the person to wear a mask. He had ceased to be the person God had created. Once the man took the mask off, the pain was revealed, then inner healing could begin. He found the real him. "He found that there was a quality of omnipotence sleeping inside of him." And so it is with you. There is an authentic person waiting and wanting to be recovered and revealed.

We all have pain and brokenness in our lives— some more than others. We sometimes allow the hurts and pains to define us. Sometimes we put on a mask to hide the pain. Many times the lies, hurts, and brokenness become a part of us. They become our "normal." Accepting this as normal can cause us to become stuck and not able to move from one level of growth to another.

This is not the true you. The word of God reads, "But you are not like that, for you are a chosen people. You are royal priests, a holy nation, God's very own possession. As a result, you can show others the goodness of God, for he called you out of the darkness into his wonderful light" (1Peter 2:9 MSG).

This chapter focuses on inner healing and its benefits. After you have forgiven others and begin inner healing work, you are propelled on your journey to becoming the you God called you to be. I share with you many benefits of inner healing, but to me, the most compelling reason is so you can develop an intimate relationship with God, Jesus, and the Holy Spirit.

Inner healing is about getting "stuff" out of your life. It is healing your heart from painful emotions. Inner healing is like taking the lid off the garbage can of life where you have stuffed pain and hurts that you didn't know how to, or didn't want to deal with it. It is peeling off the layers of pain and unpacking the baggage of your life.

Inner healing is about dealing with hidden core pains. These soul wounds can cause harm to your body. When there is an injury, abuse or, something that causes you pain or brokenness, it can then lead to anger and a refusal to forgive. This can lead to resentment which then can produce emotional and physical illnesses in your life. I'm not sure we're always aware of this process taking place.

Emotional pain can be associated with physical illness, spiritual illness, social illness, and economic illness. I have suffered from an ulcer, irritable bowel syndrome, and fibromyalgia at different times in my life. I now know they were related to the environmental and psychological stressors I was dealing with. Please note, I stated, "can be related" to emotional pain.

Weight gain can result from trying to medicate emotional pain with food. When you don't want to feel the pain, you overeat. This can lead to you becoming caught up in a vicious cycle: the pain wants to come up, you medicate with food, you then feel guilt which causes you to overeat. This is repeated over and over until you become overweight or obese. I have been caught up in this cycle and have had big weight gain over the years. Losing the weight has become a part of my inner healing journey.

If there is pain from the past and you fail to forgive and heal it, you become imprisoned while the person who harmed you has gone about living their life. Pain from the past interferes with you coming into your truest identity and reaching your goals in life. The pain keeps you from operating fully because it steals energy from you.

Inner healing allows you to get past whatever's holding you back, and to reclaim what has been stolen (or what you gave away). It allows you to get to the core of your being by getting rid of past hurts pains, and brokenness.

Most importantly, inner healing allows you to see the you that God sent to this earth. Not necessarily the you that you have become as a result of abuse, hearing hurtful words hurled at you constantly, bad choices, unforgiveness, etc. You can rewrite your script, develop a new story, and start living a whole new life once you have gone through the healing process.

You do inner healing so you can see and accept the person God says you are. It's getting pain out so you can let love in. Here is a list of what inner healing allows you to do:

- It allows you to conquer things you thought had a hold on you.
- Inner healing gives you freedom to operate in your environment. When you fear your environment, you work to control it. There is no peace for you to "just be."
- It allows you to let go of being responsible for someone else's behavior.
- Inner healing allows you to see what is normal, and what is not. You begin to see the effects of culture and family on your life.
- It allows you to see yourself as worthy. There's no longer a need to prove yourself.

- Inner healing allows you to identify and deal with the lies in your life.
- It allows you to accept God's unconditional love.
- Inner healing allows you to take responsibility for your life.
- Inner healing allows you to be, when in the past you were always concerned with doing.
- It heals your heart from painful emotions.

For me, the most compelling reason for beginning and staying on the journey to inner healing was so I could have an intimate relationship with God. When you get "stuff" out, you can truly see who God is, who He says you are, and what He has in store for you.

Many people may blame God for what happened to them as a child, as I did. They may look back on the situation and say, "God could have prevented that from happening." They attribute all the awful things that have happened to God. That is a lie from the enemy. The person in authority did the wrong, not God. You must learn to forgive and release the person to God. With inner healing, God fills the empty spaces with His light, love, joy, and peace.

An intimate relationship with God gives you freedom to be. If you don't appreciate the freedom you have in Christ, you may work hard to please Him. This can result in a sense of unrest and

121

incompleteness. You may fear that nothing you do is good enough. Romans 8:15 reads, "For you did not receive the spirit of bondage again to fear, but you received the Spirit of adoption by whom we cry out Abba Father" (ERV).

As daughters of the most high God, we experience a new identity in Christ. We are new creations with the mind of Christ. There may be times when your thoughts and your behavior don't match your new identity in Christ. This can be caused by the enemy operating in your life preventing you from your true identity. Inner healing enables you to close the door to enemy.

The lies of the enemy can cause strongholds in your life. The strongholds are first developed in the mind – in your way of thinking. Behind strongholds are lies. These lies are beliefs you hold to be true: you're stupid and can't learn; you'll always be fat; you'll never amount to anything, etc. These types of lies can become your truths and guide your behavior.

Behind every lie is fear. This fear can freeze you, torment you, make you feel powerless, and lead you to make wrong decisions. You have the power and authority in Christ Jesus to take all negative thoughts captive (2 Corinthians 10:5). Renewing your mind can bring about transformation. You must see this as a process that may take you some time to learn.

In inner healing, you learn to identify, resist and renounce the lies of the enemy. You replace the lies of the enemy with what the Father says. You tell the enemy, "I will not believe your lies because God says I am . . ." You must believe and continue to speak what God says about you. You can make declaration such as, "I am the righteousness of God and I can do all things through Christ who strengthens me."

Bringing inner healing to people was part of Jesus' ministry on earth. It's also part of the salvation plan. When Jesus went into the Temple and was handed the scroll to read, He read from Isaiah 61:1-3. Christ stated His earthly mission in this passage.

> The Spirit of the Lord GOD is on me. The LORD has chosen me to tell good news to the poor and to comfort those who are sad. He sent me to tell the captives and prisoners that they have been set free. He sent me to announce that the time has come for the LORD to show his kindness, when our God will also punish evil people. He has sent me to comfort those who are sad, those in Zion who mourn. I will take away the ashes on their head, and I will give them a crown. I will take away their sadness, and I will give them the oil of happiness. I will take away their sorrow, and I will give them

celebration clothes. He sent me to name them "Good Trees" and "The LORD's Wonderful Plant." (ERV)

Wholeness is part of the salvation plan. In 1Thess 5:23, Paul writes, "We pray that God himself, the God of peace, will make you pure—belonging only to him. We pray that your whole self—spirit, soul, and body—will be kept safe and be blameless when our Lord Jesus Christ comes" (ERV).

I believe spiritual health requires you to be emotionally healthy. Pains from the past interfere with your relationship with God. You cannot experience closeness because of pain standing between you and God. Inner healing allows you to rid of yourself of this, enter into God's rest, and recognize you are more than a conqueror through Jesus Christ our Lord.

I am sometimes saddened when I look back and recognize the effects that carrying around pain from the past had on me. I isolated myself as best I could while living in a large family. I was plagued with low self-esteem and had no sense of self-worth, and I was shy. I had no idea of who I was because the pains of the past were obscuring everything God was saying about me. They had blinded me to the true me. Making this journey has enabled me to learn who I am in God.

When I reflect on my past, I see the doors to the enemy were opened in my life. I found the enemy was busy strategizing and setting up various experiences to support the negative things I was believing about myself. Open doors are seen as entry ways into your life that the enemy uses to keep you off track. For example, anger is one way the enemy uses to get to you. When we get angry and don't deal with it, the enemy can gain access. In Ephesians 4:26-27, we read, "Be angry, and do not sin; do not let the sun go down on your wrath, nor give place to the devil."

I mentioned earlier that I had erected a wall in my life for protection. Once my wall was removed, God's unconditional love could get in. I didn't know how much God loved me and that He accepted me as I was. I began to marvel in it. This further allowed me to truly begin to understand who I was and how wonderful I am in His sight.

Inner healing enables you to erase negative demeaning tapes from your past. These negative tapes were usually recorded when the parents, teachers, and other significant adults were angry and you were a convenient target. They begin to play automatically when you experience a stressful situation similar to ones from your childhood.

These tapes from the past have played so much that many come to believe everything on them, such as:

- You're no good

- You'll never amount to anything
- You're just like your no good father
- You're bad
- You're stupid
- You're a waste of my time

It was refreshing, yet, somewhat difficult to accept that the tapes from my past didn't really describe who I was. I had come to believe the tapes because people important to my development had recorded them. I recorded new positive tapes using affirmations. I had to start saying positive things about me to me. It took me some time to learn to accept deep truths about me.

One of my daughters gave me a book on the life of Joseph years after I started my inner healing journey. I had shared my pains of the past with her, and she told me I reminded her of Joseph. The book detailed the hardships he endured on the journey to his destiny and purpose. She couldn't believe what I had come through to get to where I was. I told her God had been with me, even when I was not aware of it. I am constantly reminded of what Joseph told his brothers when he was reunited with them:

So Joseph said to his brothers again, "Come here to me. I beg you, come here." When the brothers went to him, he said to them, "I am your brother

Joseph. I am the one you sold as a slave to Egypt. Now don't be worried. Don't be angry with yourselves for what you did. It was God's plan for me to come here. I am here to save people's lives. This terrible famine has continued for two years now, and there will be five more years without planting or harvest. So God sent me here ahead of you so that I can save your people in this country. It was not your fault that I was sent here. It was God's plan. God made me like a father to Pharaoh. I am the governor over all his house and over all Egypt. Genesis 45: 4-8 (ERV)

Can you imagine what Joseph went through to get to the point where he could forgive his brothers for selling him into slavery? God's mercy and favor were on his life from the time he was sold into slavery until he was "governor over all the house of Pharaoh and over all Egypt." One would guess Joseph was willing to forgive and let go of everything that would've kept him from living the life God wanted for him.

I believe the first step to inner healing takes place when the pain of the past becomes unbearable and you know something has to happen. You must come to a point when you can admit there is a problem, you own it, and accept you can do something to change. It's time to open your heart and allow God to begin the work of inner healing.

The second step is to identify what's causing the emotional pain. Is the pain related to past soul wounds? Many wounds are from not having basic needs met in childhood. Answering this may require you to move out of you comfort zone. I shared with you earlier how I reacted when I went to my first therapist – nervous, scared, and determined to put up a strong front. You will have to visit the past as I did so you can deal with those issues that are causing you pain.

Next, you identify the false beliefs, defenses, and survival strategies you've developed as a result of the pain. A defense mechanism is something a person uses to protect him/herself against pain and anxiety. You employ one at any given time when you can't cope with painful thoughts and feelings. Some defense mechanisms you may have used to make it in your environment are:

- Denial – selective forgetting; "There is no problem."
- Minimizing – saying the situation is not as severe as it is; "It's not so bad."
- Blaming others – Not taking responsibility for your behaviors

- Blaming self – "It's my fault; I wouldn't been hurt if I hadn't done…"
- Rationalizing – Offering excuses, justifying behaviors
- Distracting – changing the subject to avoid dealing with issues
- Becoming hostile – getting angry when people bring up a topic

I believe denial is one of the most dangerous defense mechanisms people use. Someone may go through most of their life in denial. You've heard the story about the elephant in the living room. One fails to admit he's sitting there in full view. Another example is an alcoholic who may deny their alcoholism; they say, "I can quit any time I want."

Denial saves a person from anxiety and pain. Well, that's what the enemy wants you to believe. The truth is, denial affects your soul: your mind, will, and emotions. It can then affect your body and spirit. If you continue to use denial over a long period of time, you may end up having to use other defense mechanisms such as repression and suppression to push and keep the pain down.

You can learn to express your fears and other emotions rather than denying them. Many people, like myself, grew up in families where feelings were not allowed to be expressed. Therefore, it may be difficult to put a name on what you're feeling. You can begin to understand and state your feeling by getting a list of "feeling words" from the internet. The list will give you a feeling word that describes what you're experiencing. There are six basic emotions/feelings: anger, disgust, fear, happiness, sadness, and surprise. Other feelings will fall under one of the six basic ones.

One of the hardest things I had to learn was that feelings were given by God and it was okay to have them – all of them. As an adult, I learned to feel by putting a name on the emotions when they came, and then learning to accept them. Of course, it was somewhat foreign to me because I had learned to shut down when the environment became toxic.

After you've identified what needs changing, you identify healthy ways for dealing with and letting go of the pain. You need the right mindset to believe you can change your beliefs and overcome the pains. This is another place where you may need professional help.

There are different methods used for inner healing. I have used individual and group therapy, had sozos and read self-help books on my journey to my truest identity. I have used so many methods over the years to deal with forgiveness and to get to inner healing. Some I learned while in therapy and others when I was learning to become a therapist.

You can create a ritual for saying goodbye to the survival strategies you learned and used in childhood. The wounded child in you is tired and would like to rest. What I mean by that is, you are now an adult and you can learn more appropriate responses to certain situations rather than relying on the ones developed in childhood. For example, when you were a child and in a social situation where you did not know how to respond, you pretended to be angry or shy so people wouldn't talk to you. You can end this old response by learning and using good communication skills in social situations.

Since forgiveness is seen as the gateway to inner healing, I share methods that have been helpful to me. One method I used to deal with unforgiveness was letter writing. I would get legal-sized sheets of paper and write to the person, telling them how they had wronged me and its effect on me. These were long, detailed letters. I would tell them I forgave them. The letters were not mailed. They were torn into tiny pieces and burned. The relief I felt was absolutely amazing.

There is the two-chair method where you place a chair in front of you and someone you trust sits in it. You pretend that the person who has wronged you is sitting in the chair and you have an opportunity to tell them how they have hurt you. At the end, you tell them you forgive them. The person in the chair can act as a surrogate and say they are sorry and ask your forgiveness. This is not required for you to forgive them and release the pain.

One of the most powerful methods for dealing with forgiveness is a Sozo. You are asked if you want to forgive a person. The person leading the session leads you into forgiving the wrongs done. This method allows you to see how you may have formed wrong ideas about God, Jesus, and the Holy Spirit, leading you to relate to the Godhead out of misconceptions. This can prevent intimacy with God. I shared with you earlier how I gave God responsibility for what my father had done, and how it interfered with our relationship. I've had many sozos since I was introduced to this method in 2010.

Sozo is a unique inner healing and deliverance ministry, based at Bethel Church in Redding, CA. It is a powerful spiritual encounter. Sozo is a Greek word which means saved, healed, and delivered. It is used for inner healing and deliverance. The aim of the session is to get to the root cause of things interfering with your relationship with God, Jesus, and the Holy Spirit. Co-creators Dawna DeSilva and Teresa Liebscher say, "a Sozo session is a time for the Sozo team to sit down with you and with the help of the Holy Spirit walk you through the process of freedom and wholeness."

Psychotherapy (talk therapy) or counseling is another method used in inner healing. Many Blacks don't use this method because they mistrust the mental health system. There is also stigma in the community if you seek help. I have heard people say you must be crazy if you go for help. Another reason given for not seeking professional help is, "You don't put family business in the street." Some family happenings need to be exposed by placing them outside the family.

Journaling is another strategy you can use in inner healing. It may be used with other methods such as talk therapy. Journaling is used to write your thoughts down on paper. It can help clear your mind. If you journal regularly, it will help you gain insight into your behaviors, moods, and what you've been denying. It's something you do privately. Journaling has mental, creative, and emotional benefits.

When you first start journaling, you can try free-writing. You just start writing about what is on your mind, without lifting the pen or pencil from the paper. Don't be concerned about spelling, punctuation, or grammar. I attended a journaling workshop years ago, and the first assignment was to free write on a given topic. I was surprised to find I had written two pages without stopping in a few minutes.

Something else I've done over the years while healing is write, "Dear God" letters. I pour my heart out to God in these letters. I tell Him what I'm feeling, what's causing the feelings, and of course, what I want Him to do about it. The letters usually begin with me giving Him praise for His goodness. I can usually count on some relief after writing to God. He is such a loving Father who says, "For I am the Lord your God, who takes hold of your right hand, and will tell you, don't be afraid! I will help you. (Isaiah 41:13, ERV)

You need the right mindset to believe that you can achieve inner healing and be an overcomer. You must be fortified to overcome the works of the enemy, and you need God's wisdom and love to do this. Inner healing awaits you.

IT'S YOUR TURN

Are you ready to get to your core, your very essence, with inner healing? You may need to get professional help to deal with some of the pains of the past. Forgiving others usually frees you for inner healing.

I want you to make a list of issues you need to release from your life. You can ask the Holy Spirit to help you identify these areas. What are the pains still holding you back? Are you still angry with your mother who was not available for you? Are you angry with your father for harsh discipline and angry words? Hurt by a teacher who called you stupid?

The pains of the past may become entrenched in your life. It's important for you to go through the process of letting go.

My Inner Healing Worksheet

List the pain of the past	How will I work through it?

WHAT DO I DO NOW?

We dealt with forgiveness in an earlier chapter. You were to see it as the gateway to inner healing. Did you relate your pains of the past to unforgiveness? Were you able to identify any unforgiveness you've been holding onto? If you did, were you able to forgive the person and the offense? Continue to ask the Holy Spirit to reveal areas in your life where you need inner healing. Do your journaling here. You can return to the exercise often.

_____

_____

_____

_____

_____

_____

_____

_____

_____

_____

But those who embraced him and took hold of His name were given the authority to become the children of God.

John 1:12 (TPT)

Yet even in the midst of almost all these things, we triumph over them all, for God has made us to be more than conquerors, and His demonstrated love is our glorious victory over everything.

Romans 8:37 (TPT)

CHAPTER 7

IDENTITY

When you make the healing journey to your truest identity, you experience the "you" God sees; it is your TRUEST identity. He knows who you are and your capabilities. He knows your strengths and your potential. He knows who He ordained and created you to be. It's important that you know as well, and that your perspective of your identity lines up with His.

I conduct a workshop with Black women called Developing an Internal Victorious Attitude (DIVA). One of the warm-up exercises is, "Who are you?" The women are paired and are told to ask each other seven times, "Who are you?" They then introduce each other from the information they gathered. The most interesting aspect of the exercise is the comments I hear when we process the exercise.

The one comment that has always stuck with me was from a seventy-something lady who said, "I have never really thought about who I am." Her comment saddened me because many Black women may, like her, go through life never really knowing who they are. We have sometimes been defined by and accepted the definitions of the many world social systems in which we interact.

Identity answers the question, "Who are you?" It includes the way you think about yourself, the way you are viewed by the world and the characteristics that define you. When you truly know who are, you can remain the same no matter what situations you may encounter.

Your identity is formed by social and life-journey experiences. A person's identity is uniquely tied to the environment in which they are reared. For Black women, this identity is significantly influenced by racism, sexism, and classism. These factors influence what a person wants to be, and what they actually become. They also affect how Black women are seen by others. Much of your God-given energy is constantly being used to just survive in the many systems you operate in. Therefore, it's so important for you to know who you are.

There are survival strategies a person may use to adapt to their social world when how they see themselves differs greatly from how others see them. For example, in childhood, a girl may see herself as good, while a parent tells her she is bad. The child will usually do something to adapt to the difference between what she sees and what her parents see and say. She may eventually begin exhibiting bad behavior, becoming what her parents has said she is.

Other children don't become what they're called; they instead are resilient. When I look back on how I was raised, and how I ended up, I would have been labeled a resilient child. There have been many books and articles written on resilient children. They are children able to bounce back from challenges, and overcome failures and serious hardships.

I went back to college at age thirty-eight to take courses in different departments in an effort to discover what majors would interest me. I took a gerontology course in the Sociology Department. The professor and I had long discussions after class. He wanted to know about my background. I freely shared with him about how I had grown up, and my current life.

The professor knew the area I had grown up in. In miles, it was not far from the university. However, it was a long way away in so many other ways. Dr. Smith wanted to know how I had made it out of College Station. He wanted to know the factors that had influenced me, who had been my mentors, and how had I maintained a strong sense of self. He suggested, "I would be rich if I could figure it all out and bottle it for others to make it out of poverty."

It is important for Black women to keep a close watch on self because how the different world systems define you can pull you away from who you are. These systems will define you and tell you who you are. The problem is they don't know you. They don't know your story – what you have come through to get to where you are. Since they don't know you, they'll define you in ways that aren't true.

Black women in American society have been negatively portrayed from slavery to this present time. Historically, some stereotypical names for Black women were Sapphire, Mammy, Jezebel, Savage, and Angry-Black-Woman. They have also been labeled as sexually promiscuous and immoral. This was during times when they were brutally raped by slave masters. The names were meant to denigrate, and take away the humanness of the Black woman.

Today, the stereotypes are welfare queen, independent, strong, overweight, angry Black woman, ghetto queen, and money hungry. The stereotyping affects how the Black woman is perceived in the home, workplace, and community. The social status of the Black woman does not affect how she is labeled. C. Nicole Mason suggests that even the former First Lady of the United States, Michelle Obama, is one neck or eye roll from being labeled an angry Black woman.

The "Angry Black Woman" is the convenient shorthand used by those who refuse to acknowledge or recognize how layered and multidimensional black women really are. We are human. Some people misinterpret our emotions and project their own thoughts onto us.

The ultimate impact of stereotyping is that Black women attempt to refute the labels placed on them. This action is counterproductive. There is only a certain amount of energy available in the body to complete the task of everyday living.

If a person ties up the allotted energy disproving and proving, there is little left for them to define who they really are, walk in their destiny, and live out their God-given purpose here on earth. They cannot truly know who they are because the energy needed to discover that isn't available. As it stands, in the American culture, the Black woman cannot "prove" herself. She will always come up lacking.

When I was a junior faculty member at a graduate school of social work, I had to contend with lies written on my annual faculty evaluations. Each year, they got progressively worse. When I picked up my evaluation my third year, I looked at it, checked to make sure I had picked up the right one, then said, "This is not me."

Once I got home, I sat quietly and prayed. I asked God to guide me in handling the situation in the healthiest way possible. I believed the Holy Spirit was guiding me to refute the lies in the evaluations. How to do this required lots of prayer. God had chosen me to put an issue on the table before, and I believed this was another opportunity to do so.

I spent the weekend copying my evaluations – one for each faculty member in preparation for the called faculty meeting the Dean had scheduled. I put the evaluations on the table, and said, "Many of you did not look at my portfolio before completing your evaluation of me." I then read from the negative ones, refuted the lies with information in my portfolio. I then requested to be reevaluated. The group method was used for my second evaluation, which was glowing.

I believe the negative evaluations were meant to devalue me and push me off-course. I was popular with students. Each year, I was selected to hood students. My evaluation scores from students were always higher than the department's average.

The evaluations contained lies about my performance as a faculty member. I could have believed them as I had other lies in the past. The more lies you have believed from the past, the harder and longer it will take you to get up the courage to refute them. The constant use of energy to disprove lies can be all consuming. You have to make a conscious decision on how much energy you will use to refute lies. It has taken me many years, lots of tears, many therapists, sister support, and God's grace to learn how to refute lies in an appropriate manner.

I have talked to many women who weren't successful in refuting the lies told them beginning in early childhood. They believed the names they were called and the negative things they were told. The lies grow and take on a life of their own.

For example, when I was growing up, I was called a "little red heifer" for as long as I can remember. At some point, I recognized I was not a red, female cow. Therefore, I didn't believe that lie. However, I wasn't always successful in refuting some lies of childhood. These lies have had negative effects on my personhood. You may not even remember when you first heard the lies or when you first believed them. The problem is that what you believe, you tend to become.

When I was working as a therapist, one strategy I used to help clients identify and work through pain from the past was to erase and record new tapes with positive messages on them. As mentioned before, tapes are recordings from your past made when a caretaker spoke negative words during your childhood. They negatively impact your identity.

Changing your mind about these tapes and their effect on you requires that you take on the mind of Christ, and begin to believe how God sees you, rather than others. However, this change may not take place overnight. This mind changing requires a radical departure from your usual way of thinking. Don't worry, it will happen.

Just think about all the mind changing we have done in the world. For example, for centuries, people thought the world was flat. Now, we know it's round. Think of the changes in medicine, factory assembly lines, etc., all because someone changed their mind about how they saw things. They made a paradigm shift.

A paradigm shift is an important change that happens when the usual way of thinking about or doing something is replaced by a new and different way. You no longer think about things the way you have in the past. You see yourself differently. You can discover who you are, walk in your destiny, and live out your God given purpose on this earth.

For example, it's okay for a "Strong Black Woman" to change her mind and allow herself to feel pain or weakness. When you accept this, you can begin to deal with the tough issues in life differently.

In the American culture, it is very difficult for a Black woman to really be herself. This identity issue looms large in the workplace for Black women. I've experienced an inordinate amount of difficulty in the workplace. There were times when I spent energy attempting to prove who I was.

I worked in an agency serving adjudicated teens. When I interviewed for the position, the supervisor asked me if I was militant. I told him I wasn't. He then told me I had a reputation for being a militant in the social work arena. I got busy trying to convince him of who I was, someone who gave a voice to the voiceless. I said my actions could be misunderstood and that was why I was seen as a militant.

I was hired for the position of therapist and found myself constantly defending myself during my tenure at that agency. My interactions with white teens and their families were constantly questioned by the supervisor. The questions asked were: Could I get the teen and their family to talk? How did they receive me (a Black therapist), and/or did I write relevant treatment plan on the teens and their family? What was interesting was the treatment plans on Black teens, written by the supervisor, all looked the same although the teens were different.

I addressed this issue because we were submitting treatment plans that would influence the court's decision. This move created additional stressors for me. Being the only Black licensed master level social worker on the clinical staff was difficult. I eventually resigned.

I have been on the faculty of two Historically Black Colleges and Universities (HBCU's) in the past. I had to deal with gender issues at these institutions. I chaired a department with all males at one of the colleges. I would send out memos announcing meetings. They would not attend faculty meeting, do committee work, or anything I asked them to do. I was so excited about working at a HBCU, and couldn't believe the treatment I received from the male faculty members.

Sisters, have you had similar experiences in the workplace? If not, consider yourself blessed. I've talked to many sisters over the years who have shared their trials in the workplace, from service jobs to professional positions. I asked my husband if he thought I would've fared better in higher education if I had started at a younger age (I was in my late forties when I started teaching). His response was pure wisdom, "I don't think these institutions are good or healthy for a Black woman at any age."

I attended a conference, "Defending our Name in the Academy," at Massachusetts Institute of Technology (MIT) in 1994. Black women from all over the world came to discuss issues they faced working in the academy – the world of academia. I was attending the conference because I had just completed my doctorate and was very interested in teaching at a university. I wanted to hear about the sisters' experiences in the various universities. By the end of the conference, I wasn't sure I wanted to teach in the hallowed halls of higher education.

One young professor stood in the aisle to ask a question as so many did during the question and answer period. This sister was an associate professor in physics. She wanted advice on "how to maintain your sense of self while teaching in a predominately white institution."

She stated, "They want to suck out your life blood and still have you perform all your duties." One professor after another would come to the microphone to ask a question. They would begin to cry before asking the question. Then the sisters in the audience would begin to cry. There was so much pain shared corporately during the conference.

I was reminded of what Beauboeuf-Lafontant said would happen if more black women started showing their truest inner selves:

> There'd be tears, there'd be crying, there'd be screaming and then there would be healing. It's not going to be pretty and it may seem chaotic, but what comes after the rain? The sun and things grow again. And they grow in a healthy way. I think that's what would happen. We should all prepare for that moment and look forward to the day when we can all just be ourselves.

I conducted interviews with eleven Black women and asked them to talk about their role at work. All the women were experiencing an inordinate amount of stress on the job. They felt that much of it was related to race and gender. The women felt they had to prove themselves by working harder than their white counterparts. They couldn't decide whether this was a self-imposed belief based on what they thought others expected of them or not.

These women also reported they had to contend with whites being promoted ahead of them. In many instances, they would have more education and work experience than their white counterpart. The ultimate dishonoring came when someone was hired over you, then you had to train them.

Becoming secure in your identity is important at any juncture on your journey. There are tools you can employ to assist you in becoming the you God sees. You can:

- Make declarations over yourself. They will help you think, believe, and see things differently.
- Read, read, read. Read your Bible, self-help books, etc.
- Write down your vision. Identify your natural talents and gifts you will use.
- Create a vision board using pictures to remind you of what you want to achieve
- Spend regular time working on your vision
- If you've received prophetic words, review them often.

Often, I reread prophetic words given me, especially when I'm feeling stuck. I read one recently from ten years ago that ended with, "I feel like God is saying if your life were a garden, it would be full and lush. Jesus loves you and is very proud of you." Another one read, "You are amazing and He calls you Beloved." Can you imagine what these words meant to me? Prophetic words can help you become more secure in knowing who you are.

IT'S YOUR TURN

Affirmations: I Am Exercise

Affirmations are positive statements you speak that will affect your conscious and unconscious mind. They can change your thinking and your behavior. Affirmations can help you restructure what you believe about yourself and your potential. The Scriptures tell us about the power of the spoken word beginning in Genesis 1. God spoke the world into existence. The apostle James tells us about the power of the tongue in James 3.

If you grew up in an unhealthy environment, chances are you may have learned to say negative things about yourself because of what you heard constantly. These statements may have affected how you see yourself and what you could do in life. Negative statements can lead to negative thinking, which then guides your actions. You may eventually learn to live below your potential. You are going to change your "stinking thinking" with affirmations.

Saying positive things about yourself may feel strange at first because you don't believe the statements are true. Say them until you believe them, and they will begin to change how you see yourself. You are journeying to see you as God sees you. God sees things in you that you and others do not see.

Write affirmations on cards and paste them around your living space. Record them on your cell phone. Say them morning, noon and night. I am starting you with a list of affirmations that I use. You will eventually write your own list. Allow the affirmations to become a real part of your journey work. Affirmations are very powerful in helping you see yourself in a positive light.

Sample Affirmations

- I am more than a conqueror
- I am lovable
- I am fearfully and wonderfully made
- I am unconditionally loved by God
- I am chosen
- I am receiving provision from God for my vision
- I am a co-heir with Christ Jesus
- I am designed to prosper
- I am the righteousness of God in Christ Jesus
- I can do all things through Christ who strengthens me
- I am accepted in the Beloved

Create your affirmation list here. Add to it often.

1. _____

2. _____

3. _____

4. _____

5. _____

6. _____

7. _____

8. _____

9. _____

10. _____

11. _____

12. _____

13. _____

14. _____

15. _____

16. _____

WHAT DO I DO NOW?

Did you have difficulty creating your affirmation list? If you did, use the sample affirmations. What's important is you start saying positive statements to yourself. I believe that with time, you'll be able to create your list, and enjoy the benefits. Write about any difficulty you had in creating your list.

I say this because I know the plans that I have for you." This message is from the LORD. "I have good plans for you. I don't plan to hurt you. I plan to give you hope and a good future.

Jeremiah 29:11 (ERV)

Delight yourself in the Lord and He will give you the desires of your heart.

Psalm 37:4

CHAPTER 8

Destiny and Purpose

A sense of destiny and purpose is important for the journey to the Truest You. There's nothing like knowing why you're here on earth and what you are to do to propel you into your truest version of you. Your life takes on real meaning when you have destiny and purpose. There's a close relationship between the two: destiny drives purpose and purpose should drive your daily actions.

Although the two are related, there's a difference between destiny and purpose. I believe it's important to know the difference between the two. Destiny is defined as the events that will necessarily happen to a particular person or thing in the future. It is the hidden power believed to control what will happen in the future. Purpose is the reason for which something is created or for which something exists. The "why" you're here on this earth.

Destiny and purpose can be seen as God's dream for your life. It is something He has placed in you before you were born. You become awakened to and aware of destiny and purpose through intimacy with God. You can truly pursue destiny and purpose after you know who you are and Whose you are.

Another way to look at destiny is that it's your future or the pre-ordained path of your life. It can be considered something that is to happen or has happened to a particular person. Paul speaks of it this way,

> In Christ, he chose us before the world was made. He chose us in love to be his holy people—people who could stand before him without any fault. And before the world was made, God decided to make us his own children through Jesus Christ. This was what God wanted, and it pleased him to do it. (Ephesians 1:4-5, ERV)

Author and Missionary Sherri Lewis says, "When you're walking in destiny and purpose, all of heaven will back you and make your visions and dreams to be manifested." She calls this "the God Zone." Sherri believes that when you have a heart full of passion and intimacy with God, it leads you into your God Zone – your destiny.

A few years ago, while spending time with God, I was asked, "If there was just one thing you could do, what would it be?" I answered out loud, "Write." I was so surprised by my answer that I looked around to see who was speaking. I repeated my answer, "Write." When I finally realized it was me talking, I said maybe I'm in a stupor induced by the massage I had gotten earlier that day.

I couldn't believe my answer because writing had become one of my least favorite things to do since getting my PhD. I had spent many hours developing my writing skills in preparation for completing my dissertation. I went to the university's writing lab and worked with a writing consultant. God was setting me up for something great. He was preparing me to write this book, not just my dissertation.

It wasn't a massage stupor I was in. The Holy Spirit had downloaded something into my spirit man. God wanted me to write. As I mentioned previously, God had told me to write a book earlier and I didn't. I didn't know it, but this was part of my destiny and purpose. God wanted me to share my story of the healing He has allowed me to experience. He was now giving me the desire of my heart – a method for sharing how He had brought me through my journey so it could be a blessing to others. I was being given the opportunity to say, "God healed my past. This is what I did, and now you can do it.

Some people say destiny is in their hands, while others say God has planned it. Because of where I am in life, I choose to believe God planned my destiny. There is no way, no how, I would've known how to get from College Station, Arkansas to where I am now. I've come a long way, not just in distance, but also in growth.

If you say you have no destiny or purpose, ask God to awaken your ability to dream again and hear who He wants you to be and what He wants you to do. I think it would be good to get prophetic words and/or review the ones you've gotten in the past. God will speak to you. He is more than willing to tell you the plans He has for you.

Life wounds, pain and traumas from the past can also keep one from dreaming and moving into destiny and purpose. These things can cause hopelessness. You need to have faith in God and believe He can change hopelessness to hope and passion. He did it for me. I continue to be amazed at the goodness of God in my life. Psalm 73:23 reads, "Yet I am always with you; you hold me by my right hand" (ERV). What blessed assurance.

The tricks and schemes of the enemy can delay God's purpose from being manifested in your life. This can also happen when we are disobedient to God's instructions. Earlier, I wrote about my disobedience in not writing this book. You must also remember He is a forgiving God who gives you more than one chance to carry out His plans for your life. I can attest to this.

I mentioned earlier the Holy Spirit had told me to write a book about my life with the intent of offering Black women advice on coming into their Truest identity. I started writing it and then allowed the enemy to sidetrack me. I wrote everything but this book. God continued to tell me to write. I asked His forgiveness, repented and began writing again. This time with passion.

God chose me and has had a plan for my life even before the foundation of the world. There is a reason He brought me to this earth. There is something He's poured into me that has to come out; it has to be manifested. I know I'm to do ministry with women suffering from emotional traumas. So it is with you. God has something He wants you to do. Have you considered your destiny and purpose?

Life and what you have experienced wants to convince you that you have no purpose, no destiny. For example, your family of origin may have spoken word curses over you: you'll never be or do anything worthwhile, you're no good, you are not deserving, etc. These messages are powerful and can negatively influence your life, unless or until, you truly learn who you are and what you are to do with your life.

I believe you must get in touch with and know who you are before you can truly pursue destiny and purpose. How can you know who God says you are and the reason He brought you to this earth if you can't hear from Him? And can you really hear from God if there are unresolved traumas in your life?

If God has poured something in you, no one can take it away, not even you. Of course, it's up to you to recognize what you have, what it's for, then bring it to fruition. For example, in 2002, I was in Africa with a mission team. During our personal devotion time, we were to ask God, "What do you want me to do?" I heard repeatedly, *"You will use your life experiences, education, and work experience for Kingdom building."* That's quite an assignment. I do believe I'm ready to carry it out.

I have remembered those words over the years as I got more serious about pursuing purpose and destiny. What had God prepared me to do? I grew up in poverty, had a variety of work experiences, and I have a PhD. How was all that going to come together for advancement in the Kingdom? How and when was this going to happen? If I had paid attention, I would've seen God preparing me over time.

Years ago, I attended a writing workshop where we were given different writing assignments. One I really enjoyed was "Charting the Course." We were to write about changes we'd made during the course of our lives and what we had learned from them.

I wrote, "From College Station to College Professor." Here is a snippet from what I wrote.

> Little did I know the little girl from College Station with no shoes or proper clothing, and who went to school when there were no crops to harvest, would end up teaching at the university level. How did I get here? I don't know. I look back in amazement when I see

JOYCE KELLY-LEWIS, PhD, MSW

the junctures, events, and the experiences that have gotten me to this place and time."

I also loved passing on to others what I had learned, especially if I believed it would enhance their lives. For example, I went to a boundary workshop and left with lots of good information. Immediately, I began to look for venues to share it. I figured we all need to know how to set boundaries, so we don't get pulled away from what God wants us to do.

In charting my course, I discovered that I mostly got involved in activities with a teaching component. They included teaching in Sunday School, youth leader at church, and Girl Scout leader. Teaching little girls to say a pledge, complete activities for a badge, or to follow a recipe for an international dish was so rewarding. Being involved with these groups signaled the beginning and development of my different teaching modalities. With my children, math was taught during cooking and sewing classes. I loved how easy it was to teach fractions while following a recipe. Actual hands-on activities were very effective.

I was reading something I had written earlier after spending time with God. "Behold, I have poured a dream into you and it is time for us to act. Me and you: what a team! Dreaming with You is an awesome experience. Matter of fact, it can be somewhat overwhelming. I hear You say, 'I am with you.' The chains are gone you are free to be who I created you to be. You have what it takes to do what I have called you to do because I put it there. You also have provision in my presence. Remember, my will for you is that you pray always and be filled with my joy. I want you to also know I love you relentlessly. Remember all this and we will be an awesome team."

I heard about and began researching the Seven Mountains of Influence for clues on what I could possibly do to influence the world in a positive way and advance God's Kingdom. Jesus pointed out that we are to be the light and salt of the earth. And these "mountains" represent areas that greatly impact individual's lives.

The seven mountains are those influential sectors in society that mold the way we think, and they shape our culture, according to Lance P. Wallnau. The seven mountains are Economy, Government and Law, Family, Spirituality and Church, Education, Arts and Entertainment, and Business and Finance. Christians are expected to fulfill their God given assignment by occupying leadership roles in these influential spheres of society.

I realized I had been working in my area of influence all along- the family. I have worked with families in different capacities over the years. I have tutored children in schools and community centers; done therapy with parents and children; and taught children in Sunday School and camp. Currently, I conduct inner healing sessions and training, locally and in Africa.

Walking in destiny requires you to take the authority given you as a Kingdom citizen. The enemy wants to keep you from recognizing and exercising the authority given you by God. The enemy is heavily invested in keeping you weighed down with and weaken by unnecessary worries intended to pull you off track.

Don't be surprised if you have to deal with adversity as you begin walking in destiny and purpose. It will come. Adversity can cause you to question identity and God. You must muster the courage to face the adversity. When adverse conditions come, the first thought is, something must be done. You start the "doing" before you adequately assess the problem. This can make things worse. Pray and ask the Holy Spirit to guide you through assessing the problem, and reveal how to resolve it. Then you do something. That something may be doing nothing because God has said, "This battle is not yours."

When I recognize that Jesus is with me during adversities, I gain courage to go through the adversity in preparation to move on to destiny. One of my favorite Scriptures is 2 Chronicles 20:1-28. Here, King Jehoshaphat demonstrates how to deal with an adversity God's way. What is instructive in this passage are the steps the King took after he was told a great army was coming to wage war against him. They were:

1. He became afraid because he recognized there was a problem they were not prepared to handle (verse 3).
2. He inquired of God. He set himself to seek the Lord about what to do (verses 3-4).
3. He called the people together and reminded God of who He had been to His people (verses 5-11).
4. King Jehoshaphat asked God to judge his enemies; take care of them because "we have no power against them: we don't even know what to do, our eyes are upon you" (verse 12).
5. The King had all the people stand together (verse 13).
6. The King received marching orders after he was told by Jahaziel the prophet, "Don't be afraid or worry about this army because the battle is not yours. It's God's battle. He was told they wouldn't have to fight. "Just stand and watch the Lord save you" (verses 14-17).
7. King Jehoshaphat worshiped God before the battle (verses 18-22).
8. The king and his men followed the instructions given. God took care of the enemy armies. All they had to do was collect the spoils, go back

home and offer praise to God for the victory (verses 22-28).

There are so many awesome lessons in this passage. Knowing we need God because we don't know to handle a given situation is pure wisdom. Like King Jehoshaphat, you can remind God of who He is and His promises made to you. God brought you to this earth for a purpose, and He has poured into you what is needed to carry it out. It's your inheritance from God.

A key to learning how to win battles God's way is to first recognize your state. It's okay to say, "God, I don't know what to do. I'm putting this in your hands." When we come to the end of ourselves, that's when God can work. We must recognize the adversity is in God's hands.

One thing I've had to learn on this journey is to praise God before, while going through, and after the battle. Praise. You just do it. I'm not saying it's easy. What I am saying is, praise God because you are assured victory when He's fighting your battle.

God's favor is needed for you to walk out your destiny. It is God's biased kindness towards you. It has nothing to do with your performance; it has to do with God's goodness, faithfulness, and unconditional love for you. I've looked at my life through the years and see God has graciously bestowed favor on me. It's so important to recognize, receive, and give thanks for

His favor. I'm sure you can look at your life and certain situations and recognize you've had God's favor on your life. Otherwise, how would you have made it through?

Look at what the Psalmist says about favor, "For you bless the righteous, O Lord; you cover him with favor as with a shield." (Psalm 5:12 ERV). "For the Lord God is a sun and shield; the Lord bestows favor and honor; no good thing does He withhold from those who walk uprightly" (Psalm 84:11 ERV).

You also need God's grace to know and carry your destiny and purpose. I believe you have to see grace as more than the unmerited favor of God. In his book *Grace: The DNA of God*, Tony Cooke teaches on graced-based living. He says, "Grace is more than the initiation into the Kingdom. Grace has enabled me to live in a way that pleased God. It produced more and more strength, wisdom, and joy in my life. I found that old areas of fear, guilt, shame, and condemnation dropped away. Grace saves us and empowers us to live a life pleasing to God."

Graham Cooke tells us, "Grace is the empowering presence within you that enables you to become the person that God sees when He looks at you. It's literally the gift to become what God sees and knows about you in Christ. It enables one to become His perception of you." You become who God says you are.

Remember, it's important to know your purpose and destiny as you journey to your truest identity. God has placed something in you that you're to manifest in the world – that's your reason for being on earth.

IT'S YOUR TURN

Select a time when you can sit quietly and talk with God. This will be a time of talking and listening. Please start by believing and knowing God placed something in you before He brought you to this earth. Different life situations may have affected your belief that you have something special to do on this earth – something only you can do.

Now that you've finished the book and all the assignments, you likely have a different perspective on life. You are now free to dream and become who God says you are and do what He has called you to do.

It's now time for you to write your vision or dream plan. What did you discover with your talk with God? Did you get a revelation about your calling? Are you clear about what He wants you to do? You are to create a vision board that depicts your plans.

A vision board is a tool used to help clarify, concentrate and maintain focus on a specific life goal. Literally, a vision board is any sort of board on which you display images that represent whatever you want to be, do or have in your life. It's an affirmation of your dreams, goals, and things that make you happy. The vision board will help you help you narrow you desires and focus on what you really want.

171

Find pictures that represent what you heard God say about what He put in you, who is He calling you to be, and what He is calling you to do. Remember, you're developing a vision board to help "see in pictures" what you will be doing.

I have included websites that walks you through creating a vision board. You may want to create more than one board once you get started. You will want to keep the completed boards in clear sight so you're constantly reminded of your destiny and purpose.

www.wikihow.com/Make-a-Vision-Board

www.pinterest.com/vision-board-samples

WHAT DO I DO NOW?

Now that you have a vision written and you've created a vision board, I want you to put the plan into action. You need to put into action what God has called you to be and do. Attempt to do something every day that moves you closer to completing your goal. Create your action plan here.

_____

_____

_____

_____

_____

_____

_____

_____

_____

_____

_____

_____

_____

My dear friend, I know that you are doing well spiritually. So I pray that everything else is going well with you and that you are enjoying good health.

3 John 2:1 (ERV)

CHAPTER 9

Self-Care

Self-care may be a foreign term to many Black women. It was for me for many of my adult years. Historically, Black women have been taught to care for others and not themselves. We tend to put ourselves last. Self-care is something we must learn and practice for a successful journey to our truest identity.

Self-care is about things we do and don't do for our body, soul, and spirit. It is about focusing on our needs and learning to meet them. It's about knowing and maintaining your physical, emotional spiritual, mental, and economic health. Self-care could be as simple as knowing when to stop and take a deep breath, or as serious as knowing when to see a doctor. One must be intentional about carving out time for self-care.

Self-care isn't something you force yourself to do. It's not a should. It's not something that adds just another task to your already long to-do list. Some may see self-care as something that's going to cost you money and lots of time. Self-care isn't restricted to activities like yoga, long hours at the gym, or spa days.

The items on my self-care list are activities that refuel and rejuvenate me; some just take time. For example, there's nothing like sitting and watching a sunrise or a sunset. I like watching the color changes. The majesty of it all refuels me. Listening to the words of a worship song can bring me calm. Reading Psalm 23 gives me blessed assurance of having God as my Shepherd.

You can create a list of self-care activities to enjoy. Self-care is about making connections to those things that bring you joy. I'm going to share self-care activities that are important to me.

Taking care of my physical health is a self-care activity. I had to learn that preventive health had to become a priority. Each year, I create a checklist and cross off the preventive services as I complete them. Since I have diabetes and hypertension, there are additional preventive medical services I make use of like a hemoglobin A1C test to assess how well I've controlled my diabetes over the previous three months.

I have learned what is needed to be in charge of my health. If I'm going for an appointment, I make sure that I visit WebMD or the Mayo Clinic website to read and gather information so I am informed and can ask questions of the doctor. I also have a husband (retired doctor) and two doctor daughters I can talk with.

I usually write down the questions I want answered during the doctor visit. You want to leave an appointment well informed. You have a right to ask questions of doctors if you don't understand the terms they use or the treatments they're recommending. I remember being with my elderly mother when she was getting care. Doctors used their big medical terms as they told her what was wrong. She just nodded her head. I knew she didn't understand, and I wanted the doctor to know that. I asked him to explain using simpler terms. I also asked questions on her behalf.

All Black women, regardless of age, education or social class, should speak up for themselves in the medical arena, especially for preventive care. We first need to believe we have a right to good health care. When it doesn't happen, you have to ask questions, then demand proper care. This means you have to take an active role in your medical care and health prevention.

Knowing your family medical history is important when you're focusing on prevention. For example, if there is a history of breast cancer in your family, you would get a mammogram at an earlier age than most women. Preventive care for women includes:

- Mammogram
- Pap smear
- Diabetes check

- Immunization
- Colonoscopy
- Bone density
- Weight check
- Blood pressure check
- Breast self-exams

It's important to talk with your primary care physician on when to start preventive services.

I believe if Black women would educate themselves and become involved in health prevention, we can lessen the leading causes of death among us: heart disease, cancers, strokes, and diabetes. There are things Black women can do to lessen or reduce the incidence of diabetes and cardiovascular disease. For example, obesity, which is associated with high cholesterol, hypertension, diabetes, and degenerative joint disease is totally preventable. You can reduce the incidence of obesity by losing weight, exercising, and eating healthy.

When I was growing up, we didn't have access to good health care, much less preventive care. I had to learn more about the diseases and syndromes I faced and what I could do to lessen their damage to my body. For example, I learned if I lessened stress in my life, I wouldn't experience as many fibromyalgia flare ups. I lost weight to lessen the fatigue I experienced and to take stress off my joints. I now wish I had known and used information about preventive and alternative health early in life.

Although our health statistics are dismal, there is hope. Many of the diseases we suffer and die from are related to unhealthy lifestyles. When you make prevention a priority, you can change your health status. If you're overweight and want to prevent obesity, YouTube is a valuable source for teaching videos. You can select exercise videos, menus for making changes in eating, and get advice from doctors and nutritionists. There are many reputable websites where you can learn about preventive care. Remember, Christ came so you could have a healthy, abundant life.

Another type of health on my self-care list is mental health. Remember, there may be times on the journey you find yourself in difficult situations beyond your ability to solve. It's okay. Trials are a real part of life. It's what you do in these situations that matter. Early on in my journey, I didn't know what to do when I experienced something beyond the blues. Of course I prayed. In my story, I told you about the Christmas I couldn't cook or go with my family to relatives for dinner. It was different from sadness, the blues, feeling down, or grief. It wasn't just something in my head or something I could "just snap out of."

I was suffering from depression and didn't recognize it. I was tired, cried a lot, had no interest in doing things I normally enjoyed. This was happening when we had four school-aged children I was caring for. My method for dealing was to do more. Can you relate? I didn't get help early on. I had to learn it was okay to seek help from a professional.

I learned there is a stigma in the Black community about seeking mental health services. "You just don't put family business in the street." There is also mistrust of the mental health facilities in our communities. However, please seek professional help if you're experiencing many of the following symptoms:

- Feeling sad on most days
- Loss of interest or pleasure in activities you once enjoyed
- Changes in appetite—weight loss or gain unrelated to dieting
- Trouble sleeping or sleeping too much
- Loss of energy or increased fatigue
- Increase in restless activity (hand-wringing or pacing) or slowed movements and speech
- Feeling worthless or guilty
- Difficulty thinking, concentrating, or making decisions
- Thoughts of death or suicide

Be honest in your assessment. I had to become honest with myself and accept I had been experiencing many of the symptoms for years. I just learned to live with this sometimes serious medical illness until I couldn't anymore.

When I discovered I was suffering from depression, I saw a therapist. The therapist recommended I see my primary care physician to have a thorough medical examination. We wanted to rule out any medical conditions contributing to what I was going through. I also began taking an antidepressant.

Depression is among the most treatable of mental disorders: between eighty and ninety percent of people with depression eventually respond well to treatment. Talk to your doctor if you believe you're experiencing depression based on the symptoms listed above. You can also ask them to refer you for mental health treatment. Other things you can do to reduce symptoms of depression are exercise, get enough sleep, eat a healthy diet, and avoid alcohol.

With therapy, medication, and exercise, I began to be less depressed. Even after I began to feel better, I continued taking my medication and going to therapy. This is an issue for many who do seek treatment; they stop taking their medication when they begin to feel better, usually without telling their doctor. Remember, you're feeling better because of treatment.

Dentist visits for preventive check-ups is on my self-care list. Do you see dental health as a part of our overall health? I didn't. I learned about preventive dental care after I got married and could afford the visits. Growing up, we only went to a dentist when we couldn't pull our decayed tooth at home with pliers. Ouch!

If you want to participate in preventive dental care and don't have insurance or can't afford it, teaching hospitals usually have dental schools where you can get services. You will need to Google "free or reduced fee for dental care." Preventive dental cost much less than dental services such as fillings, extractions, or crowns.

One item I've added to my self-care list is soaking in a bathtub with Epsom salt. This is a simple way to take away stress and soreness. Adding Dead Sea salt and Essential oils can take the soaking to an even deeper level. Dead Sea salt is reported to contains minerals that treat skin ailments and arthritis. An essential oil is a natural product extracted from medicinal plants. They are good for mood disorders and physical ailments. I enjoy a good soak with lavender, rosemary, and peppermint.

You want to soak for 20-30 minutes. Keep the water at a comfortable temperature. The essential oils are added after you've filled the tub. You must be intentional about your soaking. I can hear you saying,

JOYCE KELLY-LEWIS, PhD, MSW

"Where am I going to find time to soak in the tub." Start by saying, "I'm deserving of it and the benefits."

Rest is an activity I added late in life to my self-care list. It took me a long time to grasp the importance of rest. I grew up in a home where rest was equated with laziness. My sisters and I joke if we call during the day and find someone still in bed. We use our mother's voice and say, "Get your lazy self out of that bed." We congratulate ourselves on the fact that we've learned to rest with no guilt.

What can I say to a Black woman about rest – especially a strong Black woman? I'll start by telling you rest is essential for the journey, and for your health. When resting, you stop movement in order to relax, refresh yourself, and to recover strength. This definition requires you to pay attention to your total well-being, especially your physical and mental state.

I remember believing I didn't have time to rest. How do I tell someone to rest who already has an overloaded to-do-list? I tell you even God rested after He had created the world. The Creator of the universe demonstrated rest on the seventh day. Now do you think you need to rest?

I'm giving you a list of benefits to further convince you to put rest on the self-care list you're going to create. Something I've found interesting about rest is it may help you discover things about yourself that you wouldn't have otherwise. Rest can help you decrease the need for stimulants like caffeinated coffee and energy drinks. You can stop pushing yourself beyond your limits if you stop to rest. Other benefits of rest include:

- Improved sleep
- A restored body
- Increased productivity
- Improved problem-solving and decision-making
- Increased alertness
- Positive feelings and an improved mood

It has been suggested rest can help you lose weight. What I know is, when I rest, and do it before tiredness sets in, I don't eat as much. I discovered I was attempting to fuel myself with food. Some of you may need to learn how to rest. I will give you an exercise at the end of this chapter that will help.

Probably, my favorite self-care activity is to get a massage. It's so relaxing and has health benefits. I've been getting massages for years. I remember I was very intentional about getting massages on a regular basis. One of my daughters was driving two hours for a visit. I told her to be there before my scheduled massage. She was late. As she was coming in the house, I was leaving. I gave her a kiss and said, "I will see you after my massage." She congratulated me for sticking to my self-care activity.

How can we talk about self-care if we don't talk about reducing stress in our lives? The Cleveland

Clinic defines stress as the body's reaction to any change that requires an adjustment or response. There are physical, mental, and emotional responses to stress. Black women as a group probably experience an inordinate level of stress because of who we are, what we do, and the care we give. Here's a quick list of things you can do to reduce stress.

- Get good rest—log off technology one hour before bedtime. Not enough sleep can make mental health issues worse.
- Keep calm and meditate/pray
- Put fast food in the rear view mirror by looking forward. What you eat can have a serious impact on how you feel. Caffeine, fried foods, rich foods can increase risk for negative responses to stress.
- Deep relaxation – Take deep breaths using a 5-7-9 count (You take a deep breath through your nose, as you push out your stomach to a count of 5. Hold your breath for a count of 7. Now, blow out the breath slowly to a count of 9. Repeat 3-5 times

Gratitude is a self-care activity that can be practiced anywhere and at any time. You can do it in the good times and in the bad times. Gratitude is a feeling, an emotion of being thankful for some benefit you've received. This positive emotion causes you to focus on what's going in your life and express thanks in response. Gratitude can improve your mood and improve your health. It can strengthen relationships when you say, "thank you" for something a person has done for you.

Gratitude is also giving thanks to God for his love, mercy, and favor. Since this source of goodness is outside of ourselves, how can you not take notice and show appreciation? The focus is on what you have, rather than what you don't have.

What I've discovered over the years is my gratitude goes to another dimension when I'm completing forms in a doctor's office. The forms contain a long list of diseases. You're asked to check the ones you have. I immediately start thanking God because there are so many I don't have. God is so good.

My self-care list tends to be long because I change activities from time to time. For example, walking is something I enjoy. When I was recovering from surgery, initially, I couldn't walk. Life situations may force you to change your self-care activities. Accept that. After having total knee replacement surgery, the doctor told me to give up tennis. I just knew I could still be able to play. I tried it one last time. The knee became swollen and painful. I gave up tennis.

The list of possible activities for self-care is endless. Some are good for your physical health, some for your soul, and some are just plain relaxing and fun.

Here's a list of possible activities. Read through it and see if anything resonates with you and strikes your fancy.

- Try a new exercise class – Pilates, HIIT, trampolining, relaxing stretch, cardio sculpting, spinning
- Take a long walk in a beautiful park
- Find a healthy meal on Pinterest and try it out.
- Invite friends over for dinner and cook together
- Find a local theatre and go see a play (You can usher if you can't afford a ticket)
- Find a DIY project that will bring something beautiful to your home or office space
- Sing at the top of your lungs
- Dance like no one is watching
- Invite a friend over to do facials with your own homemade products
- Get a massage
- Meditate to soaking music
- Learn how to do deep breathing exercises and then do them on a regular basis
- Learn how to make tasty but healthy green smoothies and incorporate them into your diet
- Plant a vegetable garden and learn to eat farm-to-table
- Take a bubble bath with jazz playing and aromatherapy candles

- Explore essential oils and see how they affect you
- Do something new and creative (whatever that looks like for you!)

There are so many things you can do to take care of you just as you take care of others. Create your own list of go-to self-care activities and then MAKE PLANS for when you'll do them. Self-care has to be intentional, deliberate, and well planned for – otherwise, it may never happen. You may have to practice the activity over and over. Build it into your lifestyle.

IT'S YOUR TURN

Are you ready to commit to better health? I hope you believe health is part of your inheritance. You can make it happen.

First, you need to identify what changes you will make to improve your health. You can then create a plan to make it happen. Write you plan on sheets of paper and place them where you see them every day. Make sure you can measure the change you want to see on your plan. Commit to the plan and watch the improvements. Let's look at a sample plan for improved sleep.

My Plan for Change

Sample

What I will change? My sleep habits – Get more than 4-5 hours sleep each night

What I will Do? Go to bed earlier. No technology in bed. Do deep breathing. Use Lavender on my pillow.

How am I doing? One week later, I'm sleeping 7-8

hours each night

My Plan for Change

What will I change?

_____

What I will do?

_____

_____

How am I doing?

_____

_____

What will I change?

_____

What I will do?

_____

_____

How am I doing?

_____

_____

What will I change?

_____

What I will do?

_____

_____

How am I doing?

_____

_____

What will I change?

_____

What I will do?

_____

_____

How am I doing?

_____

_____

Learning to Rest

I want you to think about taking a long car trip. What would you do when you tire of driving? You pull into a rest stop. I want you to think about what you find there. The items I think about are:

- Refreshments
- A parking lot so you can stop driving
- A path where you can walk and clear your head
- Restrooms
- Informational leaflets
- Someone to answer your questions

Using the car trip as a metaphor for the journey to your truest identity, I want you to make a list of items that'll help you learn to rest. For example, what music helps you relax and rest? Do you need someone to teach you how to rest?

_____

_____

_____

_____

_____

_____

WHAT DO I DO NOW?

You can become intentional about becoming healthier in all areas of your life. I wrote earlier that if one area in your life is not healthy, it can spill over and cause problems in other areas. What happens to you when you're not feeling well physically? I can tell you what happens to me: I become withdrawn (social isolation), don't pray and read the Bible (spiritual issue), etc.

Being intentional means you're constantly thinking and doing something to improve your life. There're so many little things you can do daily that will pay off in the long run. You're to discover them daily.

Create a list of your discoveries. Make plans to incorporate them into your daily activities. For example, you can do deep breathing to reduce stress. You may need to create a reminder initially. Continue using the reminder until it becomes a healthy habit.

_____

_____

_____

_____

_____

_____

The steps of the God-pursuing ones
follow firmly in the footsteps of the Lord,
and God delights in every step they take to follow
him.

(Psalm 37:23 TPT)

And we know [with great confidence] that God [who
is deeply concerned about us] causes all things to
work together [as a plan] for good for those who love
God, to those who are called according to His
plan and purpose.

(Romans 8:28 AMP)

CHAPTER 10

AM I THERE YET?

"Mommy, Mommy, are we there yet?" I usually heard these words what seemed like a thousand times when we were traveling with our four children. The problem was, the question was sometimes asked too soon after the trip started, then after thirty minutes, then fifteen, and on and on. I would get to the point of telling them, "Let me tell you when we're there."

I invited you on a journey to your Truest identity in this book/workbook. You may be asking, "Am I there yet?" after completing the book. I can't answer that question for you. What I can do is take you through a series of questions, and ask you to reflect on what you've read. Ask the Holy spirit where you are on the journey.

I also remind you of the suggestion to get professional help if you were having difficulty while reading this book and doing the exercises. Remember, I shared with you my decision to get professional counseling (lots of it) and sozos.

In the first chapter, I shared my early journey. I was authentic and transparent hoping you would gain from my sharing. I wanted you to see where I started and the struggles I championed to get to where I am today. My journey was not easy. However, I persevered to get to my truest identity and so can you.

In the second chapter, I asked you to take a look at your life; basically to do an assessment. Were you able to determine where you were as compared to where you had expected to be in life? I believe this was an important step in the early phase of the journey. What did you learn when you completed It's Your Turn? Were you surprised by your findings? Were you on or off track? I can remember how shocked I was with my findings when I did the exercise decades ago. I was so far from where I had expected to be.

When I began the intentional journey to my Truest identity, I remember the importance of honestly looking at my current status. Although I wasn't happy with what I discovered, the assessment was necessary, and very informative. Asking you to look at your present position was intended to create in you a desire for something different and new. This in turn would propel you to make the necessary changes to get there.

Were you successful in making peace with your past and forgiving yourself and others? I can't begin to tell you how much energy is released when you identify and eliminate the negatives. Can you see yourself breathing sighs of relief and walking out of the past's influence on your present? Can you see it?

You can expect a healthier you as a result of dealing with your past and forgiving those who have

JOURNEYING TO MY TRUEST IDENTITY

wronged you. I mentioned earlier how difficult a task that was for me. However, I did it because I was on a mission to get "stuff" out of my life so I could begin to see and believe truths about me. I was on a journey to see me as God sees me.

Can you be successful on life's journey without identifying roadblocks – those obstacles in your path that prevent you from becoming all that you can be? My experience has been when I can identify the obstacle, I do a better job of handling any given situation. I have to get discernment from the Holy Spirit about how to identify and deal with the obstacle.

The obstacles are sometimes like the weights mentioned in Hebrews 12:1b, "let us lay aside every weight, and the sin which doth so easily beset us, and let us run with patience the race that is set before us. This is how it reads in the Easy to Read Version, "So we, too, should run the race that is before us and never quit. We should remove from our lives anything that would slow us down and the sin that so often makes us fall, for the path has been already marked out before us.

I discovered I have a role to play in successfully dealing with obstacles so I can finish the race set before me; God has already done His part. Do your part and allow God to take care of the rest.

I presented a case for Black women to keep a close eye on their sense of self. The many internal and external obstacles you face can so easily take one off course on the journey to your truest identity. Did you identify and examine those hindrances in your life? I hope you were able to develop healthy approaches for dealing with them.

The chapter on inner healing was written to help you identify and expose the lies of the enemy and replace them with God's truth. I gave you a list of reasons for doing inner healing. The most compelling one was so you could develop an intimate relationship with God, Jesus, and the Holy Spirit. Inner healing allows you to get rid of baggage and pick up luggage. I do hope you chose one of the suggested inner healing strategies to get to your inner core.

Are you able to embrace your Truest Identity? Remember, identity answers the question, "Who are you." Knowing who you are causes you to walk a different way and in different directions. You are also freed to know you carry something special, the greatness of God. He shines in your life and you recognize you're a co-creator with Him. God wants you to shine. When you do this, you can bring heaven to earth.

Have you identified what God poured in you and how to manifest it on your journey? What is your destiny and purpose? If you haven't acted on your gifting, it's still there. Romans 11:29 reads, "God never changes his mind about the people he calls. He never decides to take back the blessings he has given them (ERV)." In The Passion Translation it reads,

"And when God chooses someone and graciously imparts gifts to him, they are never rescinded." That is good news.

It is now destiny and purpose time. I hope you've spent time with God asking Him to show you what He has called you to be and do. Have you gotten prophetic words from trusted individuals? Revisit them. Are there common themes in them? What are you hearing the Holy Spirit say?

Once you have answered the questions above, write a vision plan. Put into words the things God wants from you. Make it specific. Write it so you can determine when you're moving towards fulfilling the vision. Make it so you can measure your progress. Make sure you put completion dates in the plan. This is such an important step on the journey. There will be help for you at the end of the chapter for writing your vision plan. Your vision boards and written plan should be complementary.

You are on a journey, not trying to get to a destination. What you have done and will continue to do on this journey is learn who you are from God's perspective. Are you at the place now where you can imagine Him looking at you and calling you His Princess, His beloved, His fearfully and wonderfully made child, and someone made in His image?

Can you receive what God says about you? If not, go back and review what you wrote at the end of each chapter. Did you work through issues? Are there

JOYCE KELLY-LEWIS, PhD, MSW

some issues you still need to work on? Are there walls you need to tear down? You also need to break unhealthy soul ties in your life.

I want you to reflect on what you've learned about you while reading and working through this book. Can you develop your own list of who God says you are? That list will replace the lies and negative things you've believed about you in the past. God's description of you is the truest. There is nothing more powerful for displacing lies in your life than with what God, your Creator says about you.

I pray God will fulfill your every request for growth. That's what journey work is all about, going from one dimension to the next. You want to be a better you tomorrow than today. You want to become more and more like Christ, walk like Him, talk like Him, and love like Him.

The journey work you do should lead to your destiny and purpose, and away from world distractors - those things placed in your path to keep you from hearing who God says you are. There are and will be distractors on this journey. With the Holy Spirit's guidance, you can see them for what they are and learn to avoid or deal with them in a healthy way. That's no easy task if you attempt to do it alone. Remember, God wants you to know who and Whose you are. All of heaven is backing you in becoming.

Make use of all the tools you've learned while reading this book and doing the exercises developed for you. They were developed from my knowledge and experience of how to make necessary changes while journeying. Do you need to develop life management skills so you can be successful on your journey?

I pray God will grant you the knowledge, courage, faith—whatever it takes for you to begin this journey to wholeness. Make no mistake about it, it will take soul searching, honesty about your present state, working through pain, prayer, and discernment. You must believe you will make it through to the other side. There is so much waiting for you. The most wonderful freedom is "being the Truest You."

As a Kingdom citizen, you are to obtain and then spread blessings. I want you to see blessings beyond material possessions: money, big car, big house, etc. Although these items will be used in blessing others, I want you to look at the whole you. What are your talents and gifts? How can you use them to bless others? For example, you obtained blessings from completing this book. You can now share the story with sisters who would benefit from it. Spread the blessings by buying them a copy of this book. As I stated earlier, we need a critical mass of sisters walking out their destiny so we can heal our communities, our land.

Have you made the choice to live up to your potential? One usually can't make this choice unless you've gotten rid of baggage from the past and allowed God to replace it with luggage filled with His love, joy, and peace. Once you've been willing to unload "stuff," God is more than willing to fill you with His light so you can see the real you; the you He brought to this earth for a particular reason. Living up to your potential requires you to make choices. You not only choose to see you as God sees you, but you also hear what He has called you to do. You then choose to walk out your destiny.

Are there any areas of your life still under the influence of a lie? If so, this will prevent you from making true change. God gives you strength to displace these lies and replace them with the truths He offers. All you have to do is receive them.

Are you living a life of constant joy and peace? This lifestyle doesn't mean you don't face trials and tribulations. It means you respond to them differently. When problems do come, you recognize that you are more than a conqueror. You learn to ask God through prayer:

- How do I respond differently?
- What I am supposed to do now?
- What lessons am I supposed to learn from this situation?
- What is missing that you want to give me?

God may instruct you to take action or He may just tell you to be still because He's going to take care of the problem. What an awesome God we're in relationship with.

You were invited to go deep and uncover the pain from the past you've been stuffing. I knew this would be difficult at times. However, the work was so necessary in getting to the Truest You. Earlier, I shared with you the fear I had of dealing with my brokenness from the past. I feared I would be overwhelmed, blown away, and end up more depressed than before I started. Well, it was just the opposite. The Holy Spirit guided me in dealing with the pain, a little-at-a-time.

Since my "garbage can" was filled with so much pain from the past, I was able to take the lid off, let some pain out, and deal with it, then put the lid back on. I looked at the source of the pain, identified the lies attached to it, and then did the healing work. I'm thankful to God for the many therapists, Sozo teams and supporters He placed in my life over the years. The journey to my truest identity continues.

Still today when I'm dealing with an issue, which is usually a lie from the enemy meant to steal my joy and peace, I use techniques I've learned in the past to uncover, expose, and deal with the lie. I hope you hear from this that the journey is continuous. If you're willing, God will equip you with the tools needed to get to your truest identity.

Hopefully by now, you've began the process of getting rid of baggage- the negative stuff from your past. I know at times it was scary. The enemy wants to keep you bound so you don't reach your potential. I'm so happy you recognized the fear was from the enemy and made a positive choice to make peace with your past and move to what God has in store for you.

I want to end this book by reminding you God continues to invite you on a journey with Him. This is a journey where you are constantly becoming where Jesus is by your side, the Holy Spirit is waiting to nurture and teach you along the way. God is a good Shepherd, and He is inviting you on a journey of a lifetime. He wants you to go out on a limb with Him. He wants to take you to your truest identity.

I want to use Psalm 23 to invite you to continue the journey to the Truest Identity. This is what God provides for you along the Journey:

- Green pastures
- Still/quiet waters
- Restoration – you can be placed in a position to see you as God sees you.
- Paths of right-living
- Even when you come to scary places on the journey, God is with you there. There is no need to fear.

If you have traded in your stuff for what God offers, you are a winner. Look at what else can be produced in your life: "But the fruit that the Spirit produces in a person's life is

- love,
- joy,
- peace,
- patience,
- kindness,
- goodness,
- faithfulness,
- gentleness, and
- self-control

There is no law against these kinds of things. (Galatians 5:22-23, ERV)

I wish I could see you do your happy dance as you embrace all that God has for you. Since I can't, I'll just have to believe you're walking around with luggage filled with the fruit of the spirit, your vision plan and affirmations, and an "I can do all things" attitude.

Be Blessed!

IT'S YOUR TURN

Write Your Vision Plan

Never doubt God's mighty power to work in you and accomplish all this. He will achieve infinitely more than your greatest request, your most unbelievable dream, and exceed your wildest imagination! He will outdo them all, for his miraculous power constantly energizes you. Ephesians 3:20 (TPT)

Name:

_____

What is God asking you to do? What is the goal? (this will probably be bigger than you can imagine)

_____

_____

_____

Why is the goal important? Who will be blessed by you completing your goal?

_____

_____

What has God placed in you to carry out this vision? List your gifts and talents to carry out this vision.

_____

_____

List things you need to do to properly prepare for this mission.

_____

_____

_____

List potential problems (Obstacles) that may get in the way of you completing your goal?

_____

_____

_____

How will you deal with issues listed above?

_____

_____

_____

What is your start date?

_____

_____

_____

WHAT DO I DO NOW?

I want you to take a deep breath. Next, congratulate yourself for completing this book. This was probably no easy task. However, you did it.

I want you to continue thinking about the things you've learned while reading this book, put the learning into practice, and continue to grow along the journey. Make summary notes here about the life you want to create.

_____

_____

_____

_____

_____

_____

_____

_____

_____

_____

Works Cited

Beauboeuf-Lafontant, Tamara. 2009. *Behind the Mask of the Strong Black Woman*. Temple University Press

Cooke. Graham. 2010. The Favor Series. Brilliant Book House.

Coley, Darryl. 2002. *The Best of Daryl Coley*. Verity. https://www.allmusic.com

Cooke, T. 2011. *GRACE: The DNA of God*. Harrison House

DeSilva, Dawna and Teresa Liebscher, 2016. *Sozo-Saved, Healed, Delivered: A Journey into Freedom with the Father, Son, and Holy Spirit.* Destiny Images Publishers, Inc.

Shirer, Priscilla., 2011. *Life Interrupted, Navigating the Unexpected.* B and H Publishing, Nashville TN.

Wallnau, Lance. 2011. Turn the World Upside Down: Developing the Nations with the Seven Mountain Strategy. Destiny Image

Wikipedia, the free encyclopedia- http://www.wikipedia.com

Made in the USA
Middletown, DE
23 February 2022